THE LO~~S~~ FRA~~N~~ YOCKEY

MW01200191

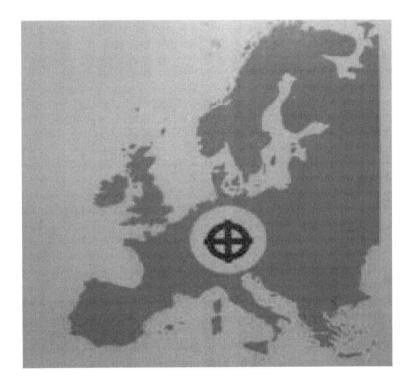

Compiled and translated by
Invictus Books

Front Cover Adolf Wamper's "Genius of Victory"

For Distribution and a list of our other titles:

Invictus Books
P.O. Box 1416
Farmington, Mo 63640
invictusbooks@yahoo.com
www.invictusbooks.com

ISBN-13: 978-0615580616 (Invictus Books)
ISBN-10: 0615580610

Table of Contents

Forward: This essay was published in August 1939 when America was still in the throes of a depression. President Roosevelt, for all of his economic schemes -- aimed at destroying the old Republic -- failed to return America to its previous productive capacity. He needed a war, and he plotted to get America into one. WW II was a victory for liberal internationalist capitalism.

THE TRAGEDY OF YOUTH
Their Generation, Now Unemployed, Must Fight the War Then Become Slaves in Red State That Follows
By *FRANCIS P. YOCKEY*

No section of the American populace has been more completely deceived by the forces interested in keeping the truth from the people than America's youth. Youth stands to suffer most from the present regime of America's enemies in control of America. Therefore, *it is from youth that the Leftist dictatorship might some day have the most to fear.*

The alien-minded minority in control of the cinema, the radio, and the newspaper and magazine press has poured out a constant stream of propaganda with the intent of gaining complete spiritual power over the minds of young Americans emerging into maturity. With what success the attempt has met everyone knows who has talked on their own level to representative American youths from the ages of 19 to 27. One and all their world-views have been cut out for them in New York, Hollywood, and Washington.

Appalling numbers of youth have been led into a cynical ultra-sophisticated attitude which regards drinking as a badge of social aptitude, which makes a fetish of sport and professes eroticism as a way of life. A perverted and insane pictorial art, lewd exhibitionistic dancing and jungle music form the spiritual norm of this sector of America's youth.

Books, Magazines Carry Propaganda

For those serious-minded youths, who are genuinely interested in the tremendous problems now facing us, another insidious attack has been devised. Books have been written, plays staged, and an unending train of lecturers have mounted the platform all to convey to these thinking youths the same message of class war and international hatred.

Magazines have been founded for none other than propaganda purposes -- *vide Life, Look, Click, Esquire, Ken, Coronet* -- and have been made up in such a way as to prove attractive to the young readers.

The result of this campaign to destroy Christian Americanism among the youth is that *every periodical, 95 per cent of the books, and all the lecturers are Leftist.* Leftist ideas are a part of the very atmosphere which American youth breathes. The young person whose reasoning powers have come to full development within the past seven years has never even come in contact with a conservative, Christian view of life. His professors are in the main Leftists, those who are not are afraid to speak out for fear of their jobs. Most of the parents do not realize the spiritual regimentation of their children because they themselves have been indoctrinated along with them. Those parents who do think otherwise are considered "old-fashioned," and proponents of the "horse-and-buggy days" by the preachers of Roosevelt Leftism.

Youth Victims of Red Demoralization

The tragedy of this conscription of American youth under the banners of atheism, class-war, and social degeneration is just this: *that the continuance of the economic and spiritual distress of the youth is an integral part of the revolutionary program of the same Communist forces which have seduced and indoctrinated them.*

According to Communist leaders, the revolutionary struggle in the United States is in the stage of the "Popular Front," with Mr. Roosevelt as the leader *pro tempore.* The aim of a "Popular Front" government can best be set forth in the words of **Maurice Thorez**, French Communist leader:

"It will be a government which will give the working-class and the Communist Party all possibilities for agitation, propaganda, organization and action, a government which will make it possible to prepare for the complete seizure of power by the working-class (i.e., by their self-chosen leaders), in brief, *a government which will be a prelude for the armed insurrection for the dictatorship of the proletariat...* For the Communists, the Popular Front is not a tactic of expediency. Still less is it an election move. It is an element of their fundamental policy, and application of the principles of Marx and Lenin ... (From his speech at Villeurbanne, January, 1936.)

Prosperity Fatal to Communist Hopes

Now it is easy to see that this program, however successful to date in America, cannot be fulfilled if our nation is prosperous arid if the population is engaged in productive, decently paid labour. Both the "Popular Front" which we now endure and its successor, *the blood-*

bath Communist dictatorship, are based on national conditions of widespread economic distress and unemployment such as we now have.

The tactic that is being employed to bring about the necessary crisis for the "complete seizure of power" is that of producing a financial collapse by profligate and insensate government expenditures on everything and anything. It does not matter whether the projects are needed or not, all that matters is that the money gets spent, and spent in such a way as to make the greatest number possible dependent on the Government, thus to break their spirits and render them fertile ground for planting class hatred, and prepare them for enrolment in the Left Army, an army which now includes labour unions, W.P.A. workers, those on relief, organized Negroes, the teachers and professors and the greater part of the youth.

The tragedy for youth lies in this, that every condition for the success of the Communist scheme is created at the expense of youth, and every tactic employed in actualizing it makes the position of youth more desperate and more nearly hopeless.

Revolutionists Do Not Want Improvement
First, there is the ghastly extent of unemployment among the youth. Hundreds of thousands of young Americans up to the age of 27 have never had any other employment than Government relief work. When will they realize that the alien-minded minority in control of our country *does not want this condition with its revolutionary possibilities removed?*

Second, the burden that the ever-growing national debt imposes is almost solely a burden on the youth. No matter how this debt is liquidated, by confiscatory inflation, or by being paid off, dollar for dollar, it will be paid at the cost of liberty and happiness of present-day American youth. If all the private and corporate wealth of the nation is confiscated to pay off the debt, what economic force will be left in the country that can run a country and employ the idle millions? And such a collapse is just the crisis out of which a Red dictatorship will fasten on America. If the other alternative is adopted, it will mean that the youth of the present will be slaves during their whole life, working, not for their own wants and happiness, but in order to pay $2 out of every $3 they earn to the Government. The national standard of living in this case would not be pleasant to contemplate.

Third, the individual future of almost every American youth has been jeopardized. Not one of those same young men now in universities and professional schools who spend their conversation in

7

deciding "how to stop Hitler" knows where or whether he can start his career.

Where is there research or construction to take up all the young engineers, business to take tip accountants and stenographers?
How many families can now afford to have a doctor every time they need one?
Or to litigate their legal claims?
Where is there a future for those trained in commerce?

Youth Always Fights the Nation's Wars

Lastly, American youth by the millions will be conscripted into armies to be sent to Asia and Europe to fight the battle of world Communism, *unless a powerful Christian nationalism arises to cast out the alien-thinking minority in Washington.* A war will give our "liberal" Government a chance to avenge wrongs done it by those foreign governments which have liquidated class war within their nations, and to defeat by a repressive war-dictatorship the incipient movement among the people against radicalism and in favour of a Christian nationalistic government.

Those to return from the battlefields where world Communism would send them to a Communist America would perhaps wish they were in the war cemeteries of Western Europe with their buddies.

With this prospect -- with the assurance of Communist leaders that the Popular Front is not only to defeat Fascism, but also to bring about Communist dictatorship -- with the mask torn off the Leftist trend of many in high posts of control in the Federal Government -- no longer controlled by Americans -- is American youth to wait supinely, absorbed in picture magazines, for the butchers to start their blood bath here?

Youth of America -- *Awake*! It's your problem and your task. You are the special victim if they win.

THE PROCLAMATION OF LONDON 1949
of the European Liberation Front
By Francis Parker Yockey

INTRODUCTION

THROUGHOUT all Europe there is stirring today a great super-personal Idea, the Idea of the Imperium of Europe, the permanent and perfect union of the peoples and nations of Europe. This Idea embodies in itself the entire content of the future, for unless this Idea is fulfilled, there will be no European future.

Those who regard this Idea, which is expressed at this moment in the Liberation Front, as a danger to them, wish to destroy it at all costs. Its enemies are, first, the anti-European forces without the Western Civilization who, at this moment of history, dominate the entire world, and second, their subservient lackeys within the Western Civilization, the reactionary party-politicians, together, with the self-interested forces they represent. Both are united in their blind hatred of this young and vital Idea, which is irresistibly releasing forces which threaten to engulf these old powers of reaction, finance-capitalism, class-war, and Bolshevism.

This is addressed to the entire Western Civilization: to the colonies planted all over the world, and to the heart and soul of the West, the Mother-soil and Father-Culture of Europe. It is Europe that is the focus of the historical force of the world. The profundity and strength of this soul and body dominate even those extra-European forces which have just concluded a temporarily victorious war against Europe, and who are now engaging in preparations for war against one another, in which each hopes to push its crude and formless lust for negative conquest even to the mastery of the world. In the plans of their masters of today, the true American people and the Russian people figure only as expendable material. In these two populations, there are wide and deep strata which inwardly belong to the Western Civilization and who look to the sacred soil of Europe as to their origin, their inspiration and their spiritual home. To these also, this proclamation is addressed.

By gigantic war, by terror, and by manifold persecution, the party-politicians and their extra-European masters have sought and seek to stifle this mighty Idea. They have sought in vain to deprive it of voice, and of all means of self-expression, through the written word or the spoken.

They themselves thus testify that the Liberation Front is already a power in Europe. Against the organic Imperative of the Front, they seek to enlist all the forces of the past. They create thus a spiritual disjunction which compels all men to take their place on the one side or the other.

It has become necessary that those who are in the service of this Idea should proclaim to the Western Civilization the spiritual foundations and significance of the Liberation Front and of the Imperium of Europe for which the Front will clear the way, for this Front is the sole creative force of our times. Therefore the representative adherents of the Front, from all, the former nations of Europe, have gathered together in London for the purpose of documenting their outlook, their aim, and their position in the world. This Proclamation is published in the original in the German, English, Spanish, Italian, French and Flemish languages.

THE HISTORICAL FOUNDATIONS OF THE LIBERATION FRONT

1. THE UNITY OF THE WESTERN CULTURE

From the beginning, the Western Culture has been a spiritual unit. This basic, universally formative fact is in the sharpest contrast to the shallow and ignorant outlook of those who pretend that the unity of the West is a new idea, a technical thing which can only be brought about on a limited and conditional basis.

From its very birth-cry in the Crusades, the Western Culture had one State, with the Emperor at its head, one Church and religion, Gothic Christianity, with an authoritarian Pope, one race, one nation, and one people, which felt itself, and was recognized by all outer forces, to be distinct and unitary. There was a universal style, Gothic, which inspired and informed all art from the crafts to the cathedrals. There was one ethical code for the Culture-bearing stratum, Western chivalry, founded on a purely Western feeling of honour. There was a universal language, Latin, and a universal law, Roman law. Even in the very adoption of older, non-Western things, the West was unitary. It made such things into an expression of its proper soul, and it universalized them.

More important than anything else, this Culture felt itself to be a power-unit as against all outer forces, whether barbarians like the Slavs, Turks and Mongols, or civilized like the Moors, Jews, and Saracens. Embryonic national differences existed even then within the West, but these differences were not felt as contrasts, and could not possibly become at that time the focus of a struggle for power. A Western knight was fighting equally for his Fatherland whether in battle against the Slav or the Turk on the Eastern Marshes of Germany, against the Moor in Spain, Italy, or Sicily, or against the Saracen in the Levant. The outer forces recognized as well this inner unity of the West. To Islam, all Westerners whatever were lumped together as Franks, giaours.

This higher Cultural unity embraced within its rich possibilities the several Nation-Ideas which were to actualize so much of Western history, for it is obviously a part of the divine plan that a High Culture create as phases of its own unfolding, not only higher aesthetic units, schools of music, painting, and lyric, higher religious and philosophical units, schools of mysticism and theology, higher bodies of nature-knowledge, schools of technics and scientific research, but also higher power-units within itself, Emperor versus papacy, Estates versus Emperor and Pope, Fronde versus King, Nation versus Nation. In Gothic times, the intra-Cultural power struggle between Emperor and Pope was always strictly subordinated, by the universal conscience, to the outer tension with the non-member of the Culture, the barbarian and heathen. The Nations existed then, but not as power-units, not as **political** organisms. The members of the nations felt themselves to be different from one another, but the differences were in no case determining of the whole orientation to life. A Slavic, Turkish, or Moorish attack on Europe was met by forces drawn from all parts of Europe.

The first political expression of Europe was in the Crusades, in which Europe was a power-unit, acting against the outer world in unitary self-assertion of its new-born soul. Alongside of this form of politics there arose the tension, which endured for three centuries within the Culture, of the twin factions of Emperor and Pope. And then from the middle of the 13th century began the revolt of the great barons and bishops against the absolute power of Emperor and Pope. This was a step further away from the prime Cultural unity, but it in no way affected the great essential idea of unity of the West *vis-à-vis* any extra-Cultural force. Thus, during this period, the Pope decreed that the crossbow was a barbarous weapon and forbade its use against members of Western Christendom, but expressly sanctioned its use against barbarians and heathens.

The increasing political differentiation within the Culture was simply the organic process of fulfilling the manifold possibilities of the soul of the Western Culture. The entire process was organically necessary, and thus divinely necessary, for the soul of a High Culture is a direct emanation of the Godhead. The development continued with the breaking of the religious unity of the West, in Renaissance, Reformation and Counter-Reformation. These phenomena, religious in origin, show us the true meaning of the political: whenever any super-personal movement or idea rises to the intensity at which it involves the question of life or death, it therewith becomes **political**, regardless of its origin in a non-political sphere. From that moment, the contestants are States, political organisms, regardless of how they describe themselves, and the way of conducting the organism is the political way: dividing the world into friend and enemy; seeking after power, and not after truth; pursuing alliance, war, and negotiation and not conversion and salvation. This is the lesson of the Reformation-centuries as it had been of the centuries of the Papal-Imperial conflict.

Accompanying the break-down of religious unity, which transformed itself into a political struggle, was the rise of the dynastic State, and the beginning of large-scale intra-Cultural wars among Western States. Again, the disunifying process within the Culture was **limited**. The intra-European wars which took place were conditioned entirely by the great Pact, felt and understood by all, that the European States belonged to the same Cultural world. Thus these wars never proceeded to the political annihilation of the opponent. They were prosecuted only to the point where the limited issue which had occasioned the war could become the object of negotiations which could satisfy both contestants.

The handing over of a strip of territory, or the recognition of an inheritance such were the limited issues of these intra-Cultural wars.

The scale of these dynastic wars gradually increased, until the dynastic form of politics itself finished, towards the close of the 18th century, when a new form of intra-Cultural power-struggle emerged.

But during the centuries of dynastic politics, with its limited wars, and its consequent preservation of Cultural unity, the other type of politics, with its other form of war, went on between Western political units and outer forces: absolute politics. These wars were unconditioned by the fact of mutual membership in a High Culture, and the presence of a common code of honour, for the barbarian and the heathen did not share the feeling of Western chivalrous obligations. The Hussite Wars, 1420-1436, show the nature of warfare between a Culture-people and a barbarian people. For 16 years, the Hussite armies flooded over large areas of Germany, burning, ravaging, killing, and destroying. This nihilistic Slavic outburst was totally unconnected with any constructive war-aim, and was thus merely an early expression of what is now called Bolshevism, the spirit of negation and destruction, wherever it manifests itself, which aims at the utter annihilation of everything Western. During the centuries of Gothic and Baroque, it was primarily Germany and Spain which protected the body of the West, and saved it from the barbarian horrors which had been its fate if the outer forces had prevailed.

2. THE AGE OF MATERIALISM

During the centuries of its growth and unfolding, the Western Culture increased in power and maturity. The inner aspects of life steadily receded before the external aspects, until by the end of the 18th century, the West stood before its deepest crisis up to that time. Since the issue was great, fundamental, and intense, it immediately became a matter of life and death, that is to say, **political**. The great crisis took political shape in the French Revolution. As ever, when an idea rises to political intensity, it absorbs everything else within it, and focuses all human attention and effort onto the power-struggle. The Revolution, however, was not French alone, but European.

This total revolution marked the victory of democracy over aristocracy, parliamentarism over the State, mass over quality, Reason over Faith, equality-ideals over organic hierarchy, of Money over Blood, of Liberalism, pluralism, free capitalism, and criticism over the organic forces of Tradition, State and Authority, and in one word, of Civilization over Culture. Rationalism and materialism were the common denominators of all the new ideas which rose in revolt against the old order of thought, State, economy, society, war, and politics. Metaphysics was to be a matter of weighing and measuring; government was to be a matter of counting noses; economy was to be entirely reduced to money-trading; the structure of society was to be a reflex of money; international relations of war and politics were to be the apotheosis of national egoism, with utter, disregard of the great, inclusive, Cultural unity, of which the nations are mere separate manifestations.

Even today, after more than a century of undermining, the traditional connections of the Culture-bearing, stratum of Europe are unimpaired, and reach straight back to the self-evident pride and mastery of our Gothic youth. And this connection is not weaker, but stronger with time, for the direction of our spiritual development has changed, and a second great world-transformation has occurred in the life the West.

We are now in the midst of the second great turning-point of the maturity of Culture. The noise and shouting of democracy and materialism have died away; liberalism has become a foul tyranny masking an evil and anonymous dictature of money; the parliaments talk now only to themselves, and it no longer matters what they say; the critics have dissolved themselves in their own acid, and cannot believe now in either their methods or their results; rapacious capitalism has eaten up its own foundations; finance has converted the nations into huge spider-webs of debt in which all Western mankind is trapped; above all, fanatical chauvinism has destroyed all the former Fatherlands and delivered them to the occupation of extra-European forces, of barbarism and Culture-distortion.

All of this is the legacy of the Age of Materialism. The servants of that Age continue to apply its outmoded and sterile methods to the living tasks of the present. But even as their dead and rigid hands grip the reins of power, the revolt continues. They cannot build a wall against Destiny; they cannot order History and Time to stop in their tracks. The assertion of liberal-capitalistic-democratic-parliamentarism that it has a timeless and eternal right to rule is an organic lie. The methods of the materialistic Age, its antiquated ideologies and cadaverous sterility, cannot even survive except as an instrument of extra-European forces, unfeeling to the inner force of European destiny.

Even as the cadaver of Materialism tries to divert the life-blood of the new and vital forces into its hardened arteries, it sinks deeper into the clammy rigidity of Death. Against this corpse rises now the upthrust of the Resurgence of Authority, the highest embodiment of the old, eternally young and manly virtues of Discipline, Responsibility, Duty, Loyalty, and Faith. In the face of the chaos of individualistic-liberal-capitalism, it flings its demand for a super-personal ethical-socialist Order. Over the equality-ideals of democracy and the chaos of national and international pluralism rises now the imperative of Hierarchy and Imperium. Displacing suicidal petty-statism is the Idea of the monolithic Culture-State-Nation-Race-People of Europe as the prelude to the greatest task of all: the expression of the absolute western will to unlimited political Imperialism.

The ultimate outcome of this gigantic struggle is known to us, for we have seen before this struggle of the Past to retard the Future. From 1800 to 1850, the reactionary adherents of the negative alliance against democracy allied themselves with the ideas and methods of the Past in order to prevent the Future. But it was the democrats of that time who represented the true idea of the times, and history does not go backward. The Holy Alliance had to fail, regardless of the material power at its disposal, for armies and cannon cannot fight against an Idea.

Within a mere century, the democrats, egalitarians, liberals, critics, ideologues and parliamentarians have become the most radical opponent of the Spirit of the Age, for this Age is no longer that of Money, Democracy, and Equality, but that of Authority, Discipline, and Faith.

No more than the Liberal-democrats could be permanently suppressed in 1850 can they suppress us in 1950. Even as the liberal-democratic tyrants bring their economic pressure, they have a bad conscience. They show it further in their vacillation between senseless cruelty and clumsy bribery, in their childish propaganda and their vain cajolery. But to the bearers of a super-personal mission, no yielding is possible, either to terror or to compromise, for this mission emanates directly from the ultimate reality of God. To the materialistic-liberal-Communist-democrats, the inner enemy of Europe, we present only one, unalterable demand: they must vanish from the face of History.

Against this inner enemy and the spirit he embodies, we now document our charges before all Europe.

In three realms, materialistic-communistic-liberal-democracy has injured the body and thwarted the Destiny of Europe: (1) within the European nations, (2) in the relations among the nations of Europe, and (3) in the relations of Europe to the rest of the world.

THE CHAOS OF THE PRESENT
A. THE UNDERMINING OF THE NATIONS

1. CLASS-WAR

In its first phase, the great revolution of nationalism and Materialism turned itself against the two poles of the Cultural life, the forces of Authority in the spiritual life and the political-social life,

Encyclopedism, Jacobinism, Freemasonry, and Republicanism are some of its early forms. They fought all signs of rank and against anything which had grown organically through the centuries. The spirit of this revolt permeated the ruling strata in some countries, particularly in France, and it was this weakness above that made the Revolution and the Terror of 1793 possible. The *canaille* never breaks loose until the ruling elements permit it; this was equally true in 1789 as in 1944, with the American conquest of Europe.

The worship of Reason applied to State and Society developed the test of quantity as the sole measure of legitimacy. Not rank, talent, genius or ability, but number alone mattered to the materialists. The source of power, according to the doctrinaire democrats was in the broadest, most undifferentiated mass of the population, and not in the spiritually differentiated strata born with the mission of accomplishing the life-task of the Nation, and actualizing the national Idea.

Blindly, the democratic ideologues continued with their work of levelling and destroying. In the century 1850-1950 they actually succeeded in undermining the State and society. What succeeded the old order? Nothing that the democrats of the early period had sought. The new centre of gravity of Life was in economics, and the dominating economic rivalry was between the industrial-capitalist and the financier. All the idealism and all the sacrifice of the egalitarians had only succeeded in wiping out an organic aristocracy and substituting for it a sordid and vulgar plutocracy. Within all countries, there now began the next form of class-war, the war between economic groups instead of between social groups. The differences engendered by quality and tradition had been undermined, and the economic materialism now supplied the cadre of forms of the struggle.

By speculation and manipulations on the exchange, the finance-capitalist attacked the productive forms of property so that they might all be working for him, the unseen and unknown master, controlling the economic life of continents through his universal network of debts and interest. The exigencies of the struggle forced the industrialists to squeeze every possible source of profit tighter, and thus to increase the already cruel oppression of the labourers and their families.

The ruling code of honour was now that of the cut-throat and the economic life of the nations was a vile scramble for profit. Into this scramble there now entered new contestants. First was the proletariat, which now allied itself with the finance-capitalist in the attack on the industrialist from above and below. The proletarian conscript was fitted out by his self-chosen non-proletarian leaders with a doctrine, organization, and tactics. The doctrine was that the entire history of the world was nothing but a continual class struggle, with money as its sole end and aim. The fact that this repulsive and grotesque outlook could even be formulated is itself the only commentary necessary on the kind of world Liberalism creates. The organization-form was the trade-union, and the tactic was the strike. All three, the doctrine, the organization, and the tactic, are entirely economic, purely materialistic and capitalistic. Although they proclaimed themselves against capitalism, they thought in its cadre, shared its aim, and fought with its weapons.

Instead of manipulating the supply of goods, like the industrialist, or the supply of money, like the finance-capitalist, they manipulated the supply of labour. The labour-leader now became the third member of the snarling capitalist trinity.

2. THE EMERGENCE OF THE JEW

More important than these domestic contestants was a new element, the Culture-alien. His entrance into Western affairs was a direct result of the victory of Rationalism and Materialism. Since only quantity mattered, then obviously the quality of a man was indifferent. The fact that he came from a different Culture, that therefore he felt himself to be a member of a different race, people, nation, State, religion, society -- these meant nothing to the doctrinaire liberals. They spoke fervently of "humanity" and wished to embrace it, little thinking that outside of the Western Culture there was no reciprocal feeling, but only sullen envy, indifference, or resentment. The liberal ideology prevailed, and from that moment the Rothschild's, Ricardo's, Marx's, LaSalle's, Bobels, Dreyfuses, Guggenheims, Loebs, Trotsky's, Stravinsky's, Krueger's, Baruchs, Frankfurters, and Blums entered into the public life of the West.

The Culture-State-Nation-Religion-Race-People of the Jew is a product of a Culture which was already completed and rigidified by the time of our Gothic period. At the time when we were just emerging from the primitive, these Culture-aliens dispersed themselves throughout Europe. Money-thinking, regarded as evil by the West, was the forte of the Jew. Interest-taking was forbidden to Westerners by their religion, and the Jew was not slow to seize the usury monopoly that this conferred on him.

In the Culture of which the Jew was a product, a nation was a unit of belief, entirely independent of the notion of territory, of Fatherland. Strewn over all Europe, the Jew naturally regarded all Westerners as alien. There was no place in the Western world of Gothic Christianity, chivalry, piety, and simple agricultural economy for this landless and uprooted stranger with his Torah and Talmud, his money and his cynicism, his dualistic ethics, one for his own kind, and another for the *goyim*. The Jew created his own ghetto as a symbol of his complete inner isolation from his environment. The general feeling of the religious Gothic Age was that the Jew was the creation of the Devil, who appointed him to drive his trade of usury.

Between the members of the Western Culture and this element which lived in and on the body of the West, but in no way shared in or contributed to its development, there arose mutual hatred and oppression. Crusaders massacred entire Jewish communities on their way to the Levant, and returning. Protests against usury produced plunder and burning of the Jews. Popes and Scholastic philosophers denounced the Jew. All Western kings, at one time or another, drove out the entire Jewish population of their kingdoms. Jews were hanged *en masse* as reprisal for their usury and counterfeiting. Any possibility of assimilation of the parasite by the host that may have been present was forever rendered impossible by the infinitely deep resentment and revenge-imperative that developed in the Culture-State-Nation-Race-People of the Jew.

Between him and his Western host-surroundings there was no inner connection. He looked upon all Western developments with an even eye, the eye of the calculating spectator who seeks solely his own advantage. Shylock is the symbol of the Jew in the Western Culture, the usurer counting his coins and accumulating his resentment. For almost a thousand years the Jew drank his gall and bided his time, and then at last his opportunity emerged. With the coming of materialism, capitalism, democracy, and liberalism, a great wave of excitement went through the Jewish world. The Jew had seen the potentialities of these things and had fostered their growth in every way. The Illuminati and all of its Freemasonic offspring were infiltrated by the Jew and made into instruments of his revenge-politics. To the Jew the great attraction of all of these Western movements was that they were quantitative, and thus all tended to break down the exclusiveness of the West, which had kept him out of its power-struggles, and confined in his ghetto, dreaming of his revenge for centuries of persecution. Henceforth, he was generously accorded the same spiritual status as Westerners in their own Culture, and the same civic status as Westerners in their own Nation-States. He kept his own exclusiveness of course, and his own public life, for the New Year's Resolutions of Liberalism -- humanitarian is in, brotherly love, "tolerance" and the like were one-sided. They were a phase of our development and could not be echoed in the Jewish organism, which had long since passed beyond all development, like the Chinese, Hindus, and Moslems.

In finance, in trade, in society, in education, in letters, in diplomacy, the Jew now forged steadily ahead, a closed organism inside an open one. While Westerners applied the test of ability, the Jew chose his associates and subordinates on the basis of their membership in his Culture-State-Nation-Race, or in one of his secret societies which extended horizontally through the Western nations.

By 1858 the Jew was able effectively to demonstrate his ability to direct the power of Western States into his channels, in the Mortara affair. During the entire 19th century, the Jew intervened constantly in the internal and external affairs of all the European Nation-States. Within each country he sought to impose the policy which would give the Jew at last the complete mastery over the Western Civilization. Thus in England, he was an Imperialist and Free-Trader, in Germany and Austria he was a liberal and social-democrat, in France he was a liberal or communist.

During the latter part of the 19th century, the Jew embarked upon an invasion of America, when the word went through the Jewish Culture-State-Nation-Race that opportunities were as great there and resistance was less, because of the absence of high traditions. In Europe, it has been impossible for the Jew to annihilate Tradition, which constantly opposed its silent and strong barrier, but in America, because of its colonial origins, there had never been creativeness and exclusiveness, and there were no barriers to the Jew. America was more thoroughly disintegrated by rationalism, materialism, liberalism and democracy than any European land, because a colony has not, and cannot have, the spiritual profundity and continuity of the Mother-soil of the Culture. As a result, the success of the Jew has been greatest in America, and in the year 1933, the entire continent of America passed into the control of the Jewish Culture-State-Nation-Race-People.

The presence of a Culture-alien generates spiritual, political, economic, and social phenomena of a kind which could never arise from domestic elements and happenings. These phenomena are manifestations of Culture-disease and of necessity arise when human groups are in contact which do not share the same Culture. When one of the groups belongs to the Culture, and the other does not -- the case of the negroes in the Boer colony, or the negroes and Indians in Brazil -- the relationship is simply **Culture-parasitism**. The disease-condition displaces Culture-members and has a slowly sterilizing effect on the Culture-body.

More aggravated is the condition when the Culture-alien intervenes in the pubic, and spiritual affairs of the host, for then he must of his own inner necessity distort the life of the host, warping and frustrating its proper tendencies to make them serviceable to his alien needs. The Jew is the only Culture-alien who at present exercises this **Culture-distortion** on the life of the Western Civilization.

The domestic disease-elements within the Culture which wish to retain the outmoded ideas and methods of the Past and to fight against the creative spirit which is actualizing a Cultural mission, are the forces of **Culture-retardation**. These have been brought into the service of the Culture-distorter. Actually these elements simply desire to lead, but are themselves incapable of leadership, and therefore devote their lives to opposition to great formative Ideas, creative spiritual currents, and leaders of vision and genius. They are the Churchill's, the spaaks, the gaulles, the rejects of higher history who offer themselves to the forces of negation and destruction. The most critical form of the disease of Culture-retardation is the condition in which it seeks to prevent the realization of the Idea of the Future even at the shame of allying with outer forces, the degradation of becoming their vassal, and the risk of destroying the entire Culture. Before showing the effect of the disease-elements on the external relations of the Culture, their internal effects must be summarized.

3. SOCIAL DEGENERATION

The forces of rationalism, materialism, atheism, Jacobinism, democracy, and liberalism became ever more radical in their demands during their century. Their most intransigent product was communism. The leading values of communism are identical with those of liberal democracy: communism also preaches the economic meaning of life, the supremacy of the individual, the sublimity of "happiness", the doctrine of heaven-on-earth, the superiority of the lowest type of man, materialism, criticism, atheism, intellectualism, hatred of authority, race suicide, feminism, and pacifism. The sole difference between liberal-democracy and communism in practice was that communism was an intensification of those beliefs to the point where they became **political**. Liberalism was anti-political, and hope to conquer with drooling sentiments, but communism was filled with an intense hatred which demanded expression in class-war.

All aspects of social decay were permeated by the Culture-distorter, who well realized their value in his programme for ascendancy. At the same time that he spread and advocated all of these forms of social decay for the White nations, he carefully strove to keep his own Culture-State-Nation-Race-People free from them. It was an invariable characteristic of the tactics of the Jew that he himself the bearer of Culture-disease, instinctively allied himself with all forms, theories, doctrines and practices of decadence in every sphere of life.

20

The degradation of the social life did not merely happen, it was planned, deliberately fostered and spread, and the systematic undermining of the entire life of the West continues today.

The instruments of this assault are the weapons of propaganda: press, radio, cinema, stage, education. These weapons are controlled at this moment in Europe almost entirely by the forces of Culture-disease and social degeneration. The chief fount of the propaganda is the cinema, and from his capital of Hollywood, the Jew spew's out an endless series of perverted films to debase and degenerate the youth of Europe, as he has so largely succeeded in doing with the youth of America. Concomitantly he inspires a vicious literature of journalism, novels, and dramas which preach the same message of destruction of healthy individual instincts, of normal familial and sexual life, of disintegration of the social organism into a heap of wandering, colliding, grains of human sand.

The message of Hollywood is the total significance of the isolated individual, stateless and rootless, outside of society and family, whose life is simply the pursuit of money and erotic pleasure. It is not the normal and healthy love of man and wife bound together by many children that Hollywood preaches, but a diseased erotic-for-its-own-sake, the sexual love of two grains of human sand, superficial and impermanent. Before this highest of all Hollywood's values, everything else must stand aside: marriage, honour, duty, patriotism, sternness, dedication of self to a higher aim. This ghastly distortion of the sexual life has created the erotomania which obsesses its millions of victims in America, and which has now been brought to the Mother-soil of Europe by the American invasion.

Not only the individuals are the victims of this technic of degeneration, but the family and the race are dissolved wherever it touches. Divorce replaces marriage, abortion replaces birth, the home acquires a purely commercial *raison d'être*, the family becomes the battleground of individual strife for personal advantage. The erotic-as-its-own-end deliberately reduces the numbers of the race, even as it also disintegrates the higher organism into sand. As a part of the technic, woman is made into a feminist, an unhappy derailed creature who would contest with man in his own domain and seek to lose all the attributes of her polarity which assure her destiny of its unfolding, and guarantee her the natural dignity which is hers. The end of the process is seen in those wide strata in America which have been completely Hollywoodized. Hollywood-feminism has created a woman who is no longer a woman but cannot be a man, and a man who is devirilized into an indeterminate thing. The name given to this process is the "setting free" of woman, and it is done in the name of "happiness", the magic word of the liberal-communist-democratic doctrine. It accompanies the spreading of inverted Puritanism, which seeks to spread erotomania by surrounding the sexual life with an aura of attractive evil.

From the standpoint of the race, the result of this technic of degeneration is the attenuating, and finally the dying out, of racial instincts. The disintegrated victims, shorn of their organic connections with the great super-personal content of Life, become unfruitful, lose their will-to-power, and soon lack the ability to believe in or to follow anything onward and upward. They become cynical, give up all inner discipline, seek a life of ease and pleasure, and sneer at all seriousness and honour. All intense feelings depart, for they might involve risk and sacrifice. Love of Fatherland gives way to money-madness and erotomania.

The complete mediocrity that results is shown by the disintegrated and unhappy Americans who were conscripted and thrown onto Europe in the Second World War. Utterly lacking as they were in any desire to fight or to accomplish even the destruction which was expected of them, nevertheless they allowed themselves to be sent abroad and killed rather than defend themselves and their Fatherland against the plans of the alien regime in Washington.

This condition of degeneration, so widespread in America, with its colonial lack of resistance to Culture-disease, and so threatening to Europe under the present American domination, has not arisen by accident. A century ago, the liberal-communist-democrat Karl Marx and his coterie formulated as their programme the destruction of the family, of marriage, and of the Fatherland. They declared a horizontal war against the Western civilization, affirming their aim of disintegrating all social, cultural, and political forms. America **is** their programme in process of actualization, and its example shows Europe what the liberal-communist-democratic regime of Culture-distortion is preparing for it during the coming generations.

But let there be no mistake: there is nothing inevitable about this Culture-disease. As long as the Culture-organism retains its traditions, its racial instincts, its will-to-power, and its natural exclusiveness and resistance to everything culturally alien, this result cannot be. The example of Quebec is proof. There, healthy instincts of resistance to Culture-disease made it impossible for the Washington regime to conscript the population of an entire third of Canada in its war of revenge, hatred, and destruction against the Father-Culture and Mother soil of Europe. The mass-heroism of the entire Quebec regiment which laid down its arms and refused as a unit when ordered to participate in the hostile invasion of the sacred soil of Europe is all inspiring proof of the presence and high potential, even in the colonies, of the invincible Western tradition of cultural purity and exclusiveness. Similarly, in the Boer colony, strong resistance was continually opposed to the war of the extra-European forces against the Western Culture. Even in America itself, the main focus of the efforts of the Culture-distorter, and the base of his great power, the main body of the people held aloof from the War in the attitude castigated by the alien regime as "isolationist". Far from being isolated, the inner soul of the true American people is connected indivisibly by the strongest possible tie, the mystical cord binding the Mother-Organism to its colony, and it was precisely because of this connecting bond that the American instinct shrank from the hateful war against Europe. It sought isolation only from the foul treason against Europe which was hatched and directed in Washington.

This great fact demonstrates to Europe and to History that America is not lost, and from this moment the Liberation Front exists also in America. The war for the Liberation of the Western Civilization embraces the colonies as well, since it is a horizontal war, like the Culture-diseases against which it is fighting. Attempts to split the West into separate units, economic, political, military, racial, are purely artificial in this age. The vertical battle of all against all belongs to the dead capitalist-nationalistic past, and its resurrection now is simply a technic of the inner enemy, an attempt to strangle the future with the dead clutch of the past. The Liberation Front, both on the Mother-soil and in the colonies, turns its back on the old vertical struggles, and opposes the Washington regime within America as totally as it opposes the puppet administrations it maintains in Europe. Within the Western Civilization itself, there are no more **real** vertical differences; the only **real** struggle of this kind in the world is the revolt of the outer world against the supremacy of the European race.

In the sphere of national economy, Culture-disease pursued during the materialistic age the same programme of destruction which the liberal-communist-democratic Marx had enunciated for it. Communist-democratic literature demanded crushing income and inheritance taxes in order to destroy the industrialists and transfer the wealth to the finance-capitalist, whose wealth is invisible, and cannot be found or taxed. In a century-long battle the forces of disease almost completely succeeded in destroying any propertied groups with Western traditions whose ascendancy itself represented a barrier to degeneration and conquest by Culture-distortion. They brought in the device of huge anonymous financial structures, called holding companies; they made the currency of nations a function of their banks, and enforced the principle of constant flux on the national economy, in order to create the possibility of financial coups.

The corrosion of Culture-disease affected not only the forms of society and economy, but those of government as well. Where once the State had stood, speaking authoritatively for all, the focus of respect and the source of order, they introduced the chaos of ideologies, each claiming to have the formula for millennium, the secret of building the old Testament promised land, in each case purely materialistic and economic. They did not speak of a World-Idea, of the Western mission in the world, of the construction of the Imperium of the West, but of trade, distribution, and the exchange. The soul of Western-man was to them a function of imports and exports, of shipping and book-keeping, of possessing and non-possessing, of rivalry between classes. The World-Mission of the West they understood as the securing of markets and raw materials overseas.

Where Authority bad stood, clothed with dignity, they now brought in gabbling parliaments, wherein the gabble became ever more meaningless, and the sham ever more patent. For these deputies are mere things, replaceable units describable only mathematically, in aggregates. Among them there is not, and cannot be, a strong individuality, for a man, a whole and entire man, does not sell himself like these parliamentary whores.

To replace the authoritative principle of public responsibility Culture-disease has brought in the anonymous irresponsibility of the decision of the amorphous majority, which can never again be found after it has committed its treason to Europe. To complete the destruction, the lying fraud of so-called elections tries to re-convince the European peoples every few months that somehow they govern themselves. Between the lies that the candidates offer the populace, and the commitments they make to their real masters, there is not the slightest connection. The programmes submitted to the electorate are compounded out of old liberal-communist-democratic ideological material, long-since historically dead. To these creatures without honour, character, or even bare understanding, the future is to be simply an extension of the past. To talk of new organization is to talk about a bigger and better parliament, of a league of nations with a gigantic parliament, bringing possibilities of higher prices for greater lies. Only the scale is to be raised. Even in England, the birthplace of the parliamentary idea, and the only place where it even had dignity and value, the idea is completely dead. With a sound instinct, the population dubs the local parliament the "gas-house". Everywhere in Europe, the populations show what they think of this putrescent fraud by insulating themselves from it: they close their ears against the programmes and the lies, they hate the ideologies, they boycott the elections, they despise from their souls the entire old-Testament Tower of Babel which today has the temerity to call itself government, and to ask for the confidence of the peoples.

This is the world that the inner enemy, the liberal-communist-democrat, has created, working with, and often under the very direction of the Culture-alien, the State-Nation-People-Race-- Society of the Jew. With their disease of Culture-retardation, with which they would strangle the future of Europe, they have reinforced the diseases of Culture-parasitism and Culture-distortion which are the gift of the Jew to Europe.

They have brought in materialism, atheism, class-war, weak happiness-ideals, race-suicide, social-atomism, racial promiscuity, decadence in the arts, erotomania, disintegration of the family, private and public dishonour, slatternly feminism, economic fluctuation and catastrophe, civil war in the family of Europe, planned degeneration of the youth through vile films and literature, and through neurotic doctrines in education. They have sought to rot Europe, to attenuate its racial instincts, to devirilize it, to deprive it of honour, heroism and manliness, of the sense of its World-Mission, of its sense of Cultural unity, even of its chivalrous military code. They have sought to paralyse the will of Europe and destroy its will-to-power by bringing in the ethical syphilis of Hollywood to poison the sacred soil of Europe.

This we lay to their charge. Those things are facts, and nothing in the future can ever eradicate the knowledge that they have been done and attempted by the inner enemy. Nor is this the full extent of the destruction wrought by the hatred, negation, and revenge of the enemies of Europe. This is the devastation **within** the peoples of Europe. It remains to document their effect in the sphere of the mutual relations of the nations of Europe, and lastly, in the sphere of the relations of Europe to the outer world.

B. THE DESTRUCTION OF THE POLITICAL UNITY OF EUROPE

During the dynastic period of Western history, although intra-European wars were of large-scale and long duration, they were limited into their aim, and the exploitation of victory was strictly conditioned. They were not national wars, but dynastic wars. Power was the stake, but only power within the prevailing forms of chivalrous ethics, comity, and Cultural unity. This unity was known as the Concert of Europe, and the very name itself reflects the deep sense of unity throughout the European family.

With the coming of the Age of Materialism, and the assault on all the traditions of the West by the forces of liberalism, Jacobinism, democracy, money, and rationalism, the dynastic concept of the Nation-idea slowly broke down and was replaced by the linguistic concept of the nation. The mystical-authoritative symbol of the ruling house had been the ultimate expression of the Nation-Idea for centuries, but now a new age demanded a new form of the nation-concept to reflect the materialistic outlook of the 19th century. Materialism thus created the linguistic test of nationality.

The increasing expansive tendency of the Western organism had resulted in a vast increase of the Western population, the reflection of its more extensive life-task. From this arose huge economic systems, stronger States than any that had previously existed, larger-scale wars, and constant increase of the power-content of the struggle.

The literary concept of the Nation-Idea, isolated the nations from one another, and accentuated their national feelings *vis-à-vis* one another. Out of this arose the distorted patriotism called chauvinism, or jingoism. It invaded the universities, the world of letters, the cabinets, and the political parties. It concentrated all of its hopes, feelings, ideals, and understanding onto the nations, and in its last stage, it finally attained to the ridiculous idea that nations are the creators of culture, that, thus, there were as many Cultures in Europe as there were nations. Since it had been the feeling of Culture unity which had bound Europe together, and had kept its internal politics and wars limited and chivalrous, this insane form of nationalism was striking at the very basis of the unity of Europe. If, in a war between two European States, each one regarded itself as a Culture, then the opponent was a **total** enemy, and the struggle was an **absolute** one. This new concept of war and politics governed the minds of the materialistic democrats and liberals, who now welcomed the jingoist into their republic of destruction. The jingoists reinterpreted the entire Past in terms of the 19th century nations. They spoke of these, nations as though they had always existed, and were mechanically and causally necessary to the existence of the world, as if they were the sole units of higher history, and as if the future, as well the past, belonged to these historical building blocks.

But once more, the materialistic assault was not entirely successful. Tradition did not break down completely, because it is the very core, the wrapping of the soul of the Western Culture. Thus, after the Franco-Prussian War, late in the 19th century, Bismarck saw to the safety and honourable treatment of the defeated French Emperor, and the treaty of peace was in the 18th century chivalrous style. The vertical nationalism of materialistic jingoism did not succeed in destroying entirely the feeling of Cultural unity, and the proof is in the Western reaction to the Chinese Boxer Rebellion in 1900. As one, the European nations joined, together with the American colony in sending a joint expeditionary force to represent and protect Europe as a unit, under the command of the German Field-Marshal Waldersee.

The struggle between Tradition and vertical nationalism continued and finally reached its highest intensity with the *caesura* of the First World War. But suddenly, with the end of that war, there was a new world in existence. Europe, in that powerful tremor, had entered upon a new phase of its existence. The break was just as profound as that of the Revolution of 1789, the other great turning-point in recent European history. The old notions of materialism nations, society, history, Politics, State, war, culture, education, ethics, science, were all swept away. In their place was a new, complete, organic view of life. Its relation to the old materialist-rationalist-democratic-communist view is most easily understood, not as true to false, but as the Future to the Past. The old materialistic, disintegratory, atomistic, liberal-parliamentary view of the world had simply died a natural death. This is the only way historical Ideas can be overcome, the organic way, by complete fulfilment and death. The First World War itself was a creation -- the last independent creation -- of that old outlook; it was the highest expression of vertical nationalism and the age of materialism.

Out of the death of the age of materialism came the new values. First, in the realm of economics, the favourite preserve of the liberal-communist-democratic gentry, the old ethical principle of capitalism yielded to the new principle of ethical socialism. Instead of the cut-throat code of every man for himself, and the concept of life as a ruthless Darwinian competition to get rich, there arose the new code of each man for all, the feeling that the State is the custodian of the destiny, and thus, of the power, of all within it that the aim of Life is not to get rich, but to actualize one's self and one's possibilities within the higher organism. Instead of the supremacy of economics and individualism, the subordination of economics and the integration of the individual into the super-personal life. The good conscience and theoretical foundations of *laisser-faire* vanished.

In the spiritual realm, atheist materialism slowly began to recede from its heights and to yield to a renewal of true religious feelings. In philosophy, sensualism gave way to the historical method, and the organism of the Western Culture throbbed anew with the rediscovery of its unitary destiny and its mighty Imperialist mission in the world.

In the sphere of Society, opposing the chaos of atomism, feminism, disintegration of home and family, race-suicide, and universal decadence, arose the idea of race-ascendancy, fertility, the preservation and integration of society, the return to social health.

The idea of the State resumed its pristine sway in the realm of politics, and parliamentarism, with its chaotic train of election, programmes, utopias, and corruption, took its place among the archaic things. The attempt to use legalism to deprive the European organism of life was overthrown, and the European will-to-power increased. The political life intensified, pacifism disappeared, European man oriented himself to the coming absolute wars for the survival of Europe, and against the outer forces.

After more than a century of constant disintegration, division, and disunification, of a constant crisis arising from the autopathic Culture-disease of rationalist-materialism, the Culture came back once more to health and soundness, to Authority and Faith. The provisional form of the restoration of Europe to health and unification of Europe was gradually assimilated by the countries of Europe, one after the other.

In the First World War, the Rationalism and Materialism, of the 18th and 19th centuries had won a pseudo-victory over the Resurgence of Faith, Authority, and Imperialism, which are the spirituality of the 20th and 21st centuries. The Culture-retarding elements which exploited this victory strove to perpetuate the old ways and ideas. With their capitalist-parliamentary league of nations they accentuated the pluralism of the States of Europe, just as they continued within each State to accentuate social-economic pluralism. The difference now was that these States were not true political units, but merely remnants which had to unite if the organism of Europe were even barely to survive. The attempt in this situation to perpetuate petty-statism and vertical nationalism was treason to Europe and to every petty-State within Europe as well. But treason is the profession of Culture-disease elements; their only acquaintance with Europe's grand Imperialist mission in the world is as with an enemy. When they see something great arising, they resolve in their crooked and envious souls to thwart it and to tear it down.

Thus it is that they resolved to destroy the European Resurgence of Authority, with its reborn Faith, and its high task of uniting the European organism for its World-Mission. When in 1936 the four leading powers of Europe signed a pact forever renouncing war among themselves, and thus affirming their European unity, the Future of Europe seemed forever guaranteed.

But in the outer world, hostile developments towards Europe far transcended the efforts of the inner-disease elements, the liberal-communist-democrats. For in America in 1933, the Culture-State-Nation-Race-People of the Jew had seized the total power, and the entire resources of America were at his disposal in his mission of hatred, revenge, and destruction of the Western Civilization, and in particular of its heart and soul, the European organism. By poisonous propaganda, by bribes on an unprecedented scale, by the purchase of whole governments and parliaments, by financial manipulations with European currencies, and by economic pressure, the Culture-distorting regime of Washington split Europe into two halves and began to prepare a World War against Europe. The instrument of this preparation in America was the monster Roosevelt, who made of his life a study in infamy, and whose name is synonymous with the pinnacle of Jewish power in the world. The Jew and his Roosevelt accomplished what no inner force in Europe ever could have attained, the creation of an unnatural and inorganic war of destruction and terror against Europe which at long last succeeded in its negative aim. The re-union of the European organism is temporarily frustrated, the Resurgence of Authority is temporarily halted, the power of every one of the former States of Europe is reduced to nil, the power of the European organism in the outer world is gone, the prestige of Europe is overshadowed by extra-European powers.

This is the new Europe, the creation of Liberal-communist democracy, the Europe of rationalist-materialism, of proletarian-Marxist-finance-capitalism, of class-war and vertical nationalism pushed to their limits. From the one direction comes the Jew, dragging in his train his nervous unhappy American victims, with their self-appointed task of "educating" Europe; from the other direction, at the invitation of and with the assistance of the Washington regime, comes the barbarian flood of the Moscow Red Army into the heart of Europe.

Where yesterday the Resurgence of Faith and Authority had stood up to open the way into the European Future, where the will-to-power, to order and achievement, to plenty and to beauty, had gone calmly ahead with its work, today the hysterical legalism of excited Jews and dead liberals enforces a grisly and monstrous terror against the peoples of Europe. Replacing the one will to unit and power, there are now a multitude of parliamentary houses where every day the soul of Europe is bought and sold, and where the economic existence of European humanity is treated as an entry in the ledger of the American foreign ministry. The triumphant disease-elements have destroyed the stability and the order of the economy of Europe, and have brought in universal poverty to replace the security and plenty which are Europe's right. With their disintegration, cut-throat capitalism, petty statism, senseless competition, and canonized selfishness, they have created want and insecurity, hunger, malnutrition, unemployment, despair and suicide. When they hang the chain of economic dependence on America around our necks, they expect a song of gratitude from the peoples of Europe, who have known independence and grandeur, but who have never known slavery.

This also we lay to their charge. The disease-elements of liberal-communist-democracy, the inner enemy of Europe, have sought to destroy permanently, and have temporarily brought low, the Cultural unity of Europe, which served to unite all the peoples through the superior Cultural bond, holding them, even in war with one another, to chivalrous usages, mutual self-respect, and political restraint. They have done it, and they cannot explain it away for these results have flowed of necessity from their inverted outlook and their dishonourable methods.

Nor is this yet all: with its social degeneration of more than a century, with its undermining of the Cultural unity of Europe by intensifying the petty-statism, chauvinism, and vertical nationalism, the coalition of Jewish Culture-distortion and liberal-communist-democratic Culture-retardation has accomplished automatically a third result, namely in the political relationship of Europe to the rest of the world.

C. THE DESTRUCTION OF EUROPE'S WORLD-EMPIRE

In 1900 the affairs of 9/10ths of the surface of the earth were ordered directly from European capitals. This was the World-Empire of Europe. This empire was the basis of the power, the security, the prosperity, yes, the very existence of Europe's peoples. In reality this Empire was simply and solely **European**, and its superficial organization as a collection of empires -- French, English, German -- was only **apparent**. But the internal tension created by petty-statism was generating a centrifugal tendency within the European Empire, and extra-European forces were exploiting this tendency. In particular, a revolt was spreading among the coloured races. The only way the great World-Empire could maintain its world-strength was by firmer integration in order to uphold its mastery and reverse the diffusion of power.

The final proof of the organic unity of this World-Empire was the fact that no single European Nation-State could injure the power of another European Nation-State without at the same time injuring itself in an equal or greater measure. But this ruling organic fact was ignored, and the tragedy of the First World War, the creation of the

Culture-retarders, the chauvinists, jingoists, and vertical nationalists, was the price Europe paid for the presence of Culture-disease. Any coloured or extra-European troops whatever that fought in this war were fighting against all Europe. Any extra-European fleets that participated were fighting the sea-power of Europe.

The demonstration of these organic facts was the new situation created by the war. The English fleet, the chief upholder of European power on the seas of the world was defeated by the extra-European sea power of Japan and America. The new arbiters of the destinies of the earth-ball were the extra-European forces, Japan, America, and Russia.

Before the First World War, Russia had figured as a Western State. Its ruling strata, its ruling outlook, were Western. The tension which existed between the Western elements of Russia and the Asiatic will-to-destruction underneath was however strained to the breaking point by the First World War, and the Asiatic elements, in conjunction with and assisted by the Culture-State-Nation-Race-People-Society of the Jew all over the world, gained the upper hand and re-oriented Russia against Europe. From then onward, and also today, 1950, Russia figures as one of the leaders of the coloured revolt against the European race. But European possibilities still exist within Russia, because in certain strata of the population adherence to the great organism of the Western Culture is an instinct, an Idea, and no material force can ever wipe it out, even though it may be temporarily repressed and driven under.

The First World War showed, to those who did not know the difference, the mutual independence of military and political Victory. Thus, although Russia was defeated in the field, it emerged from the war with increased power and voice in the affairs of the world. Japan, which took no military part in the war, was a leading political victor. Although England was supposedly victorious in the fight it lost its power in the Pacific to Japan and America, its power in the Western Hemisphere to America, its naval hegemony to Japan and America, and its world-prestige to the coloured revolt against the European race. The European-English Raj in India was completely undermined by the war, and the successful Indian Mutiny in 1947 stems directly from the First World War.

But the Culture-retarders had not finished their work. They had found a Europe which controlled 9/10ths of the surface of the planet. With their suicidal war, they had reduced the empire to the point where it controlled 2/10ths of the world, but their destructive potentialities and instincts were not yet exhausted. They formulated a league of nations to strangle Europe and to admit the entire world into the direction of Europe's internal affairs; they asserted their system of degeneration, destruction and death was the **legal** system, and that it could never be changed. Law does not exist to express and to serve life, no, these liberal-communist-democrats said that **Life** exists in order to serve the **Law**. This old Testament legalism determined to forever prevent Europe from rising again out of the general defeat of the First World War and from reconquering the world-domain which belongs to it by virtue of its strength of will, its organizatory ability, its necessity of self-expression, its irrepressible instinct, its Destiny and its Faith. Here, as always, the various forms of Culture-disease showed their natural affinity. The Culture-distorting Jewish State-Nation-Race supplemented the efforts of the Culture-retarders to hold Europe down and back, to strangle it economically, and to force the dispersion of the European populations over the earth as despairing poverty-stricken, futureless emigrants.

All the disease-elements united in the negation and hatred of the great European Resurgence of Authority. The conquest of the savage negro landscape of Abyssinia by the European race was diabolically represented as a "crime" by the Jewish democratic-liberal-communist disease. While the soul of Europe throbbed with renewed hope and vigour at this manifestation of its old eternally-young reassertion of its will and its Destiny, the disease-elements embarked on the preparation of a treacherous and dishonourable war forever to destroy the European World-Empire, the European homeland, the soul of Europe, and the high Destiny of Europe.

They sought to open the war in European Spain in 1936. Russian Bolshevism sent agents and arms, Hollywood-American Bolshevism sent military and financial assistance, Jewish Bolshevism sent leaders and organizers. The liberal-communist-democratic gang all over the Western world, the inner enemy of the West, waxed enthusiastic, and from their ranks flowed a stream of conscripts on their mission of destruction. But Europe reacted as a unit and frustrated the Bolshevik-trinity of the outer enemies.

The next attempt was on the European frontier of Bohemia in 1938. Again, the four leading units of Europe mutually joined to prevent the destruction of the Empire and organism of Europe. Therefore, the next assault was more carefully prepared and preceded by a thorough organization of the Culture-retarding elements for the supreme treason of creating a Second World War in the form of a senseless struggle within the European organism. All the world knew that such a war, if prolonged, could only ruin the European Empire and every people and province of Europe. Even the traitors knew it in part of their souls, but a traitor is wilfully blind. Treason is nothing but incapacity when it becomes resolute. If it had not been clear to them before the war, it was made clear during the war. The Architect of the War, the crypto-Culture-distorter Roosevelt, expressly stated his two war-aims to his Churchill's as the destruction of the German State and the English Empire, the two halves of the body of Europe, the foundation and the edifice of the European Empire.

This was their Second World War. It was made possible only by the treason of the inner enemy, the liberal-communist-democrat. No force within the Western Culture could even think of opposing successfully the powerful wave of Destiny sweeping through Europe, the Resurgence of Authority and the will-to-Imperium. But in their crooked, dark, and jealous hatred of greatness and grandeur, the liberal-communist-democrats, the class-warriors and finance-capitalists, the materialists and parliamentarians, called in the outer forces, the Bolshevisms of Washington, Moscow, and Tel-Aviv, and invited them to do the destruction to which they were not equal. Chauvinism and jingoism were merely techniques, and they could not inspirit any Europeans. The burden of the fighting was borne by the extra-European forces, for European troops simply were not equal spiritually to a contest against the organism of Europe.

The very tactics of the war were in the pattern of negation and hatred. The extra-European forces, led by the Culture-distorter, evolved the principle that the purpose of warfare is to destroy the civilian population of the arbitrarily-chosen enemy. The industrial life of Europe was unimpaired, the armies were intact, but the American-Jew and the Jewish-American continued their war against homes and families, while the forces of Asiatic Russia carried on the real, the military war. The warfare of revenge and hatred from the air was a deterrent to the military victory of the American-Jewish synthesis, but that did not matter, for their mission was not political **victory**, but total **destruction**, destruction of the Culture-People-Race-Society of Europe. Thus, the military assistance to Russia was not on a political basis, but was given recklessly, without any thought to the future, because the Washington-Tel-Aviv alliance was not even thinking of increasing its own power or of building a world-empire for itself, but simply, solely, and only, of destroying the Empire, the organism, and the Destiny of Europe. Consequently, American-Jewry negotiated a generous peace with Japan, which recognized the victory of the Japanese mission in the Orient and in the occupation of Japan, a policy of friendship, benevolence and reconstruction was put into effect. Their exploitation of victory was in the same twisted and crooked pattern as their own souls. Their great, compulsion is the inversion of every truth and the perversion of all higher life.

At the beginning of their efforts to create the Second World War in the form which they gave to it, they found a Europe which was master of its own territory and ruler of 1/5th of the world. At the end of their war, they were able to survey the Europe of their own creation. Europe stripped of its world-empire and occupied by extra-European forces, economically dependent on them as a slave upon his master.

In this Europe of liberal-democracy, the enemies of Europe proceeded to exploit their victory. Drunk with their power they began to kill *en masse* those who had opposed them and who had devoted their lives to furthering the Destiny of Europe. Even in murder, they could not be straight: they had to find Old-Testament reasons, legalistic rituals, to mask their murders. They invented, and sought to engraft onto the Culture of Europe, the device of the scaffold-trial. They revelled, they gloated, they prolonged their greatest Mosaic trial of all for a year. They sought to humiliate their victims in life by every imaginable meanness, and in death they thought to deprive their victims of historical rank by the hateful and stupid trick of distributing their ashes over the landscape. They tore into shreds the chivalrous traditions of treatment of war-prisoners, and twisted the Geneva Convention out of shape by assorting it gave them power to hang any soldier as a criminal who had opposed the victory of the American-Jewish-liberal-democratic forces. The more they widen their Mosaic ritual of trial-killing, the more transparent it is to Europe that it is two worlds which are here in front of one another, and that this conflict cannot be settled in an Old-Testament courtroom, but will grow and continue, deepen and intensify, until the Culture-alien is expelled totally and finally from the sacred soil of the West.

Their terror includes every land of Europe, despite their pretence that it is isolated. The trick of showing a smiling face to part of Europe and concentrating the hostility onto another part of Europe deceives no one. As long as the Culture-retarders who administer Europe remain docile, accept American food rations, service American investments, and receive American garrisons, the Washington regime will smile. But Europe has seen the other face of the American-Jew and the Jewish-American, devoid alike of sympathy, wisdom, and policy, cruel, sneering and stupidly arrogant. This attempt to divide Europe might perhaps succeed if the feeling of comradeship were absent from European populations. But a thousand years of Cultural unity, of the same experiences in every realm, of the same sufferings, even at one another's hands, has united the Europeans indissolubly. They know it now more than ever before, for they have learnt it anew under the Jewish-American lash.

Lastly, we lay to the charge of the inner enemy that he has destroyed the World-Empire of Europe with his vertical nationalism and petty-statism, and by his vassalage to the Bolshevism of Washington, Moscow, and the Culture-State-Nation-Race-People of the Jew. He has thus destroyed the power of every European State, and has turned over the soil of Europe to outer enemies.

III. THE MISSION OF THE LIBERATION FRONT

Europe knows the identity of the inner enemy and that for which he is responsible. It knows that he is the worst enemy of Europe, because he masquerades as a European, but Europe has outer enemies toward whom also it must adopt a definitive position.

The outer enemies are the Bolshevik regime of Moscow, the Jewish-American Bolshevik regime of Washington, and the Culture-State-Nation-Race of the Jew, which has now created a new centre of intrigue for itself in Tel-Aviv, a secondary New York.

The outer enemies are today the arbiters of Europe. They have set up their alternative to the natural, destined Europe of Authority and Faith: Europe as a source of booty for extra-European forces; Europe as a reservoir of man-power for the disposition of the American generalate; Europe as a loan-market for the New York financier; Europe as a beggar-colony watching for crumbs from the table of rich America; Europe as a historical sight for visiting colonials, a place where once there were great happenings; Europe as a museum, a mausoleum; Europe as a moribund collection of petty-states and squabbling peoples; Europe as an economic mad-house where every tiny unit is against every other; Europe as a backward population waiting for re-education by the American world-clown and the sadistic Jew; Europe, as a laboratory for gigantic social experiments by Moscow and for the genocide experimentation of New York and Tel-Aviv; Europe as a Black Mass of scaffold-trials, backward-looking persecution, treason, terror, despair and suicide.

And a mere fifty years ago, Europe was a proud independent organism, sure of itself and master of the world. The sacred soil of the Western Culture is now occupied by the Mongols, Turkestani, and Kirghizians of Asia, by the Negroes of America, the Senegalese of Africa, the Jews from the pavements of the world. This is democratic Europe, liberal Europe.

But these conditions are only external, material. The soul of Europe cannot be occupied, ruled, or dominated by Culture-aliens. Only a materialist could think that the possession of the tangible appurtenances of power guarantees the eternal continuance of power. If that had been so, a few castes and States would have always ruled the world, from its beginning. But, in the ultimate test, power is the reflection of inner qualities, and these qualities are not possessed by any of the outer enemies of Europe. Their transitory empires are built on sand, because underlying them there is no super-personal soul, no World-Mission, no World-Idea, no Destiny. Even in our short lives we have seen empires come and go, and the temporary power-agglomerations of Moscow and Washington will go the same way.

The outer enemies of Europe are doomed just as the inner enemy is. Time is against the inner enemy, because History cannot go backward, even if for a short time backward-looking dotards may try to force History to share the death-rattle with them.

And so with these crude and heterogeneous things that the Moscow barbarian and the Washington Jew like to think are empires. They will vanish like the morning mist under the bright rays of History. The Future belongs only to those who have the Inner Imperative to actualize a World-Idea latent in them, and there is only one source of this Imperative. It cannot be invented artificially, it must be organic, and no man or men can make it. It derives from the basic cosmic-spiritual origin of the universe, itself, derives from God.

Thus, the Liberation Front now states to Europe its two great tasks: (1) the complete expulsion of everything alien from the soul and from the soil of Europe, the cleansing of the European soul of the dross of 19th century materialism and rationalism with its money-worship, liberal-democracy, social degeneration, parliamentarism, class-war, feminism, vertical nationalism, finance-capitalism, petty-statism, chauvinism, the Bolshevism of Moscow and Washington, the ethical syphilis of Hollywood, and the spiritual leprosy of New York; (2) the construction of the Imperium of Europe and the actualizing of the divinely-emanated European will to unlimited political Imperialism.

Replacing the Culture-disease of extra-Europeans and traitors are the pristine ethical values of Europe: Authority, Faith, Discipline, Duty, Order, Hierarchy, Fertility, Will-to-Power.
This Proclamation is thus a Declaration of War.

In this War, the Liberation Front speaks for Europe, it represents Europe, it is the custodian of Europe's Destiny. It is thus clothed with the mantle of super-personal invincibility that is the attribute of the European organism. No massacres, and no scaffold-trials, no terror or persecution can touch this force; the cannon and bayonets of Washington cannot harm it, but in the end it will dissolve them. It will drive the Jewish-American forces into the seas; it will throw the Asiatic armies of Moscow back into the remoteness of Asia.

In this struggle, all the former peoples, races, and nations of Europe coalesce, for in the beginning the war is solely a horizontal one:

Race now means, in Europe, the duality of having honour and pride;

People means the we-feeling of all Europeans;

Nation now means the organism of Europe Itself.

English, German, French, Italian, Spanish -- these are now mere place-names and linguistic variations. Like all of the other rich products of our great Culture, they will continue but they are no longer political terms. Local cultures in Europe may be as diversified as they wish, and they will enjoy a perfect autonomy in the European Imperium, now that the oppression of vertical nationalism is dead. Anyone who seeks to perpetuate petty-statism or old-fashioned nationalism is the inner enemy of Europe. He is playing the game, of the extra-European forces; he is dividing Europe and committing treason.

Treason now has only one meaning to Europe: it means serving any other force than Europe. There is only one treason now, treason to Europe. The nations are dead, for Europe is born.

The Liberation Front does not allow Europe to be distracted by the situation of the moment, in which the two crude Bolshevisms of Washington and Moscow are preparing a Third World War. In those preparations, the Culture-retarders, the inner enemies, the liberal-communist-democrats are again at their posts: with one voice the Churchill's, the spaaks, the lies, the gaulles, croak that Washington is going to save Europe from Moscow, or that Moscow is going to take Europe from Washington. There is nothing to substantiate this propaganda. **The fact is that only American intervention in the Second World War prevented Europe from completely destroying Bolshevik Russia, as a political unit.** The present Russian Empire is thus the creation of America. Never in the 500 years of Russian history has Russia been able to make its way unaided into Europe. It invaded Prussia against the great Frederick only when aided by France, Austria and Sweden. It invaded France in 1814 and 1815 only when assisted by England, Austria and Prussia. It invaded Europe in 1945 only by the help of America. Russia is only a threat to a divided Europe; a united Europe can destroy the power of Russia at the moment of its choosing. It is a crass lie to say that Europe cannot defend itself against Russia. Do they think it is possible for Europe to forget the knowledge that it has just purchased with the blood of millions of its sons? Do they believe that Europe can forget that the Jewish-American regime and it alone, brought the Red Armies into the heart of Europe?

Is it possible that they think that Europe can forget that the inner enemy with his liberal-communist-democracy led Europe into this abyss? Europe remembers, and it knows the liberal-democrat as the creature of the abyss, the spirit of negation who seeks an ever-lower abyss. He destroyed a world-Empire, and now he asks for the confidence of Europe for a new crusade.

Washington's programme is to conscript the Europeans -- what it cynically calls the "man-power" of Europe -- and thus to spare the jitterbugs of North America the losses of arduous campaigns against Russia. Abysmal stupidity motivates this wish-thought. Do they really think that Europeans will accomplish military wonders fighting against one enemy of Europe on behalf of another? Do they think an American-Jewish High Command inspires the feelings necessary in a European officer-corps to elicit its heroic instincts?

No, Europe is no more interested in this projected war than in a struggle between two negro tribes in the Sudan.

The European struggle is the fight for the liberation of our sacred soil and our Western soul. It is a horizontal struggle, against all enemies of Europe, inner enemies and extra-European forces, whoever they are. Before Europe can fight a vertical war, it must be constituted as the Imperium of Europe, the organic Culture-State-Nation-Race-People of the West. And when Europe makes war then, it will, be against the political enemy of its own choosing, and at the time of its choosing. In these decisions, Jew, Moscow, and Washington will figure not at all. The propaganda of the American-Jew and the Jewish-American deceives no one. With their talk of a struggle between "East" and "West" they hope to entice the marginal minds of Europe into cooperation with them. But to us, the West is a word containing a divinely-emanated Mission, a sacred word, and it does not refer to America, to Russia, or to the Jew, but solely to the sacred soil of Europe and to the European organism.

All extra-European forces on European soil are enemies to precisely the same extent and in exactly the same degree. Europe will never fight for any extra-European force; Europe will never enter into any relationship in which it is not master; the outcome of wars between extra-European forces is a matter of indifference to the future of Europe.

The crude power structures of Washington and Moscow have no Past, and therefore no Future. They are without Tradition, without a World-Mission, without a Nation-Idea, without a Destiny, without organic unity, without a State, and without Imperial possibilities. Both of these formless things are mere pale caricatures of the one, true,

World-Mission, which inheres in Europe alone. This Mission does not arise from human will, but is a direct emanation of God.

In this great struggle for the Liberation of Europe, every European of race, honour, and pride belongs with us, regardless of his provenance. The only Europeans outside of our ranks are the Culture-traitors, the disease of our Age. The Liberation Front itself is the provisional form of the European nation, and it will endure until the permanent form of the European Imperium is established.

In the mission of the Liberation of Europe, the exact date of final accomplishment is secondary to us, precisely because we know that our victory is already determined.

With every decade, every year that goes by the European will to the perfect union and full flowering which are its Destiny becomes stronger. Our will is unbroken, our resolution stronger than ever a European resolution before us. With massive calmness we enter upon this greatest of all tasks to which ever European men have dedicated themselves.

Against the bayonets and cannon of the extra-European forces we oppose a will harder than their steel, which will wrench their weapons and their power from their grasp.   With contempt we will grind the inner enemy into the dirt.

A millennium of European history, of joy and sacrifice, of heroism and nobility, impel us to our task. To the blood that has flowed on the sacred soil of Europe we shall add the blood of our enemies. We shall continue until Europe is freed from its enemies, and the European banner floats over its own soil from Galway to Memelland and from North Cape to Gibraltar.

Europe Awake!

Two Reflections

By *Francis Parker Yockey*
Thoughts, Distilled from a Memorandum Written in June, 1950

The world-situation of the moment takes the form of war-preparations between the two remaining powers. Such a war would be a great war, and would be begun with corresponding caution. No "incident" in Berlin, Trieste, or elsewhere could precipitate such a war.

It is obvious that neither power is prepared. Preparation means something quite different to both powers. To Russia it means a much higher state of TECHNICAL organization, for America's sole advantage VIS-À-VIS Russia is the technical one. To America it means possessing of vast masses of infantry. Both powers will need years of preparation. I do not mean absolute preparation, for that never exists, but only the feeling of preparedness.

The stake of the war will be possession of the soil of Europe, the center of the world.

Russia can win only with higher technical development; America only with infantry-masses far greater than it alone can raise.

To urge a crusade against Moscow Bolshevism simply plays into the hands of the Washington regime.

Imperialism now supplants the older word fascism. Fascism was still infused with petty-stateism to a greater or lesser degree.

The enemy is organized INTERNATIONALLY on all levels. For us to fail so to organize is to insure that our several struggles, however gallant and heroic, will be severally doomed. It is simply the reign of terror in Europe that keeps Europeans out of active politics and in their homes.

By the ordinary cycles governing such things, it can be known that in about five years, approximately 1955, the initiative will pass to us, for us to exploit, or to throw away.

October 1953

All of the intellectuals and critics who have read Spengler

almost without exception have misunderstood him. They missed the highly important sentence: "What I have written here is true, that is, true for me and for the leading minds of the time to come." These scholarly idiots all put the question to themselves: Is this philosophy TRUE? Naturally in an age of criticism, nothing is considered subjectively true, as all the scholars, again almost without exception rejected Spengler, although all borrowed his method and his terminology and conclusions in great part to reach philosophical conclusions in perfect harmony with the Pollyanna spirit of 1900.

Any one of the XXth century who thinks that the philosophy is objectively true or objectively false is an anachronism, and an idiot. A belief is true if it makes us more efficient, more dangerous, and more coordinated. In this sense Spengler is TRUE – his philosophy corresponds to our deepest metaphysical instinct, make us thus harmonious in feeling and in deed and in word.

The scholar-idiots demonstrated also in their senseless fault-finding with Spengler their total incompetence in the esthetic realm: a philosophy is a PICTURE – here again, Spengler said it for them, but this they did not read, and if a picture is a WHOLE, if it LIVES, if it WORKS CREATIVELY on the observer, it is esthetically true. It does not matter whether in the foreground the shadows fall right and left in the background.

We live in an age when mental refinement, like everything else rare and beautiful, has apparently died out. The statesmen are miserable self-seekers, almost without exception, the so-called thinkers are merely erudite mouthpieces of the party-politician, the scientists are fakirs who change their theories every few years, there are no religionists, no artists, no universal minds here.

WHAT IS BEHIND THE HANGING OF THE ELEVEN JEWS IN PRAGUE?

By *Francis P. Yockey*
Published in December 1952

On Friday, November 27, there burst upon the world an event which though small in itself, will have gigantic repercussions in the happenings to come. It will have these repercussions because it will force a political reorientation in the minds of the European elite.

That event was the conclusion of the treason trial of the Jews in Prague, and their condemnation to death. During the years 1945 and 1946 the coalition Jewry-Washington-Moscow functioned quite perfectly and frictionlessly. When the Israel "State" was established as the result of armed Jewish aggression, the entire world, dominated by Moscow and Washington, sang hymns of praise and congratulation. Washington recognized the new "State" *de facto* within a few hours of its proclaimed existence. Moscow outbid Washington in pro-Jewishness by giving *de jure* recognition. Both Washington and Moscow vied with one another in seeking to please the Israel operetta-state and aided it by all means moral and material. Russian diplomats boasted that at last, in Haifa, they had a warm-water port.

And now, after a few short years, Israel is recalling its "ambassadors" from Russian vassal-states, and intensifying its anti-Russian policy from its American citadel. Volatile Jews in Israel and America cry out that Stalin is following in the footsteps of Hitler. The entire American press boils with fury at anti-semitism in Russia. Anti-semitism, warns the New York Times, is the one thing America will not tolerate in the world.

Why this bouleversement?

It began early in 1947 with the Russian refusal to surrender a part of its sovereignty to the so-called "united nations" for purposes of "control" of the atomic weapon industry. Jewish statesmen, being materialistic in their metaphysics, believe strongly in the "absolute" military power of atomic weapons, and considered it thus indispensable for the success of their policy that they control these weapons unconditionally. This control they already possessed in America through the Atomic Energy Commission, specially created and constituted so that it is beyond the reach of Congress, and responsible only to the President, who is, by the practical rules of

American inner-politics, an appointee of the Culture-State-Nation-People-Race of the Jew. They sought the same degree of control of atomic weapons in Russia, and used the device of the "united nations" to submit an ultimatum to the Russian leadership on this question.

This was in the latter part of 1946, when the tide of atom-worship was at its height, and the minds of nearly all of the poor crop of statesmen who today conduct the political affairs of the world were fantastically dominated by a mere explosive bomb. A similar mania reigned for a short time after the invention of dynamite, after the invention of the machine-gun. The Russian regime also believed in atoms with the same religious faith, and thus regarded the abdication of its "atomic" sovereignty as equivalent to the abdication of its entire sovereignty, thus the Jewish-American ultimatum in late 1946 was rejected, and in early 1947 the preparation for the Third World War began.

This Russian refusal stymied the plans of the Jewish leadership, which aimed at a surrender of both Russian and American sovereignty to the "united nations", an instrumentality dominated by the Jewish Culture-State-Nation-People-Race. Even supine, politically-unconscious America could hardly be expected to give up its sovereignty when the only other world-power unconditionally refused, and the entire policy had to be scrapped.

The next policy of the Jewish leadership was to persuade the Stalin regime by the encirclement and pressure of the "cold war" that it was hopeless to resist. The same tactic was used against the regime of Adolf Hitler from 1933 until 1936, when war was decided upon at the earliest feasible moment.

Because of the Russian rejection of the atomic weapon ultimatum, Russia now found its policy opposed everywhere, in Austria, in Germany, in Korea, in Finland. Those same American publicists who had become so deft at explaining Russia's need for "security" as Russia seized one landscape after another, suddenly turned against Russia the accusation of "aggressor". The faithful Russian servants in the West, like Truman, Acheson, Churchill, Attlee, Gaulle and the rest became suddenly -- almost -- anti-Russian. Naturally they did not use the same sort of language against Russia, the peace-loving democratic people of yesterday, that they had used against Germany, and -- naturally again --- they did not yet use the language of "Unconditional Surrender" when it came to a military test, in Korea. Although they had eagerly sought Russian aid against Germany, they did not now seek German aid against Russia. That would be going too far, and it is one of the political weaknesses of the Jew that he is the victim of *idées fixes*. The leading obsession of the

Jew is his unreasoning hatred of Germany, which, at this present stage of Europe's cultural evolution means: unreasoning hatred of Europe.

For several years there have been grumblings and undertones in the American press against "anti-semitism" in Russia. These dark mutterings began after the Russian rejection in late 1946 of the Jewish-American ultimatum on the atomic weapon question. It was then that the Stalin regime began its inner-policy of dropping its numerous Jews from the highest positions, then working on down to the lower positions. Elastically, the Stalin regime tried all approaches to the Jewish leadership: it offered aid to Israel; it withdrew the offer and shut off emigration to Israel; it tried every policy, but still the Jewish-American encirclement policy continued. Wooing the Arabs did not change the mood of the Jewish-American leadership, nor did spurning the Arabs. The press campaign against Russia continued in America and all its European vassal-states. "Russia is anti-semitic" -- thus thundered the American press, and, as political initiates know, this is the worst epithet in the American arsenal of political invective. As Eisenhower said, when accused by Truman of being an anti-semite: "How low can you get?"

The treason trials in Bohemia are neither the beginning nor the end of a historical process; they are merely an unmistakable turning point. Henceforth, all must *perforce* reorient their policy in view of the undeniable reshaping of the world-situation. The ostrich-policy is suicide. The talk of "defence against Bolshevism" belongs now to yesterday, as does the nonsense of talking of "the defence of Europe" at a period when every inch of European soil is dominated by the deadly enemies of Europe, those who seek its political-cultural-historical extinction at all costs.

That same barbaric despotism called the Russian empire and presided over by the fat peasant Stalin -- Djugashvili, who rules by his cunning a Khanate greater than all those gathered together by the mighty Genghis, is today the only obstacle to the domination of the entire earth by the instrumentality called "united nations". This vast Russian empire was created by the Jewish-American hatred of Europe-Germany. During the Second World War, in order to prevent Stalin and his pan-Slav nationalist-religious entourage from concluding peace with Europe-Germany, the Jewish-American leadership gave Russian military equipment in unheard-of masses, and political promises, gifts and advantages with unheard-of largesse. With the 14,795 airplanes; 375,883 trucks; and 7,056 tanks given it by America, Russia occupied all Eastern Europe for itself, and advanced into Magdeburg, Weimar and Vienna. The American Secretary of State Marshall acted consciously and openly as a Russian agent in undermining the Chiang regime in China and delivering quietly to Russian vassaldom a quarter of the world's population. It was only later that this conduct of Marshall's seemed reprehensible; at the time, he was regarded as a distinguished diplomat, like Churchill and Roosevelt at Teheran, and was decorated for his service to Russia.

Gradually the picture changed, there was more talk of "anti-semitism" in Russia, and American public opinion, in prompt and unconditional obedience to the American press, switched over from being anti-German and pro-Russian to being anti-German and anti-Russian.

The epoch marked by the trials in Prague is not absolute; Russian papers still explain that the Jews condemned to death for sacrificing the interests of Bohemia to the interests of Jewry were "enemies of the Jewish people". The American Jewish Committee takes the same line, so that people elsewhere in the world, in places like America and its English appendage, will not develop the idea that it would even be possible for a Jew holding public office in a host-country to behave like a Jew, and not like a loyal member of the host-country. The American Jewish Committee, however, gives no explanation whatever, not even in mere words, of what possible reason Russia would have for charging loyal Russian subjects with sacrificing Russian interests to Israel interests. They give us no clue. Apparently they would have the world believe that the canny peasant regime of Stalin is embarking on entirely unmotivated adventures in the same realm of world-politics which destroyed the political power of National Socialist Europe; the power of the Jewish Culture-State-Nation-People-Race.

The question of "guilt" or "innocence" in these, or any other political trials, like the stinking horror of Nürnberg, is historically meaningless. The Jewish victims in Prague, like the Rosenberg's in America, merely did not understand how late it was in the development of the "cold war". The fashion of yesterday, of being pro-Russian in word and act, has changed. The Rosenberg's were not *au courant*. The Jewish officials in Prague also were living in yesterday and felt far more secure than they were. In 1952 they behaved as though they were in 1945.

Anyone who knows the simple meaning of the world "politics" knows that these trials were not spontaneous outbreaks of "race prejudice" on the part of politically wide-awake Stalin and his power-hungry entourage. These men want power and they will not attack on a front where, in the event of victory, no power could possibly be gained. For 35 years, Stalin has been pro-Jewish in his inner- and outer-policy, and if he now changes, it is for well-considered reasons of state-necessity.

The same Jewish press which says Stalin is "anti-semitic" says that his Jewish victims are "enemies of the Jews". If they really believed this of his victims, the trials show that Stalin is pro-Jewish, not that he is anti-Jewish. However, nothing is easier than to catch the Jewish leaders in contradictions during these times when they are frantically realizing that perhaps their atomic ultimatum, their "united nations" front against Russia, their "cold war" encirclement of Russia and their Korean war were gigantic blunders.

Up to now their objective within Russia has been to replace the Stalin regime, which the Jews consider as a traitor to the fundamental principle of Bolshevism, by a new Trotsky. Just as they constantly hoped for an internal revolution in Germany, so they have hoped for a revolution against Stalin, a revolution to return to Trotskyism and the fundamental principle of international Bolshevism, a revolution to wipe out religious, pan-Slav Russian nationalist-imperialism, a revolution which would embrace the "united nations" and bring about a Jewish millennium, the reunion of Baruch and Kaganovich, of Lippman and Ehrenburg, of Buttenwieser and Eisner, of Ana Pauker and Ana Rosenberg. But now, this hope has vanished. There is no way of bringing about the millennium by peaceful means, through coercion of Russia by "cold war" and "united nations".

It is possible now to record the developments which have been rendered inevitable by the clear break signified by the Prague trials.

First, and most important of all to those of us who believe in the Liberation of Europe and the Imperium of Europe: this is the beginning of the end of the American hegemony of Europe. The shoddy structure of Morgenthau Plan and Marshall Plan, of Schumann Plan and Strassburg Plan, of the American flag flying over European capitals, of NATO, of the systematic subjugation and spoliation of Germany, of the satanic project of constructing a German Army to fight Russia on behalf of the occupying Jewish-American enemy, an Army without a General Staff, officered by democrats and armed with the weapons of 1870, the whole prolonged democratic holiday of Churchill's, gaulles, spaaks, gasperis, adenauers and schumanns. For Europe, the Prague trials will act as a historical cathartic to flush out the historical waste-matter of Churchill's and their liberal-democratic-communist dirt.

The American hegemony is doomed because all Europe realizes with a start -- what Imperium, The Proclamation of London and the Frontfighter have preached for years -- that the power on whose behalf Europe is asked to fight, "Bolshevism" is none other than the Jewish State-Nation-People-Race, that entity which itself is the historical creator and leader of political Bolshevism.

It is obvious that events which were strong enough to force Stalin to reorient his entire world-policy and to become openly anti-Jewish will have the same effect on the   Europe.

In the dark days of 1945, many Europeans embraced the American occupation as the lesser of two evils. During the past 7 years the comparative destructiveness of Russian barbarism and American-Jewish Bolshevism has appeared in its true proportions, the proportions set forth in Imperium, Volume II: a Russian occupation would be far less dangerous to Europe because of the abysmal cultural gulf between Russian and the West. This   gulf   would   render impossible the erection of a vassal-state system, because there are no religious pan-Slavs in Europe, and the Russian barbarian leadership trusts no one else. The notion -- fostered by wild American propaganda -- that Russia could kill off the 250,000,000 people of Europe need not be taken seriously. It is a vile insult to European spiritual resources and masculinity, as well as being a historical nightmare and originated no doubt in the brain of some American writer of science-fantasy stories.

For political purposes, and increasingly for total cultural purposes, America is dominated absolutely by the Culture-State-Nation-People-Race of the Jew. America in Europe appeals to all the forces of Culture-Retardation and reaction, the forces of laziness and degeneracy, of inferiority and bad instincts. From the spiritual sewers of Europe, America can siphon up an endless number of Churchill's to do its dirty work of dividing, despoiling and destroying Europe in a suicidal war.

Henceforth, the European elite can emerge more and more into affairs, and will force the Jewish-American leadership to render back, step by step, the custody of European Destiny to Europe, its best forces, its natural, organic leadership. If the Jewish-American leaders refuse, the new leaders of Europe will threaten them with the Russian bogey. By thus playing off Russia against the Jewish-American leadership, Europe can bring about its Liberation, possibly even before the Third World War.

A second inevitable development from the turning-point of the Prague trials is the intensification of the American diplomatic offensive against Russia, the "cold war". The press campaign will intensify in America and in Europe; Russia will become morally blacker and blacker; the American armament will be accelerated; all potential soviet agents will be liquidated by the "united nations". Russia will naturally retaliate: today Pravda says "Zionism is a tool of

American imperialism". Tomorrow it will say: "American imperialism is the tool of Zionism".

A third inevitable development: the collapse of the American-Jewish position in the Near East and throughout Islam. Since Russia will be unable to retreat from its anti-Jewish policy and the Jewish State-Nation-People-Race from its anti-Russian policy, since for each one there is no other power-opponent in the world, Russia will *perforce* ally itself with Islam, and Islam will *perforce* ally itself with Russia. Dark clouds of tragedy are gathering over the operetta-State of Israel, with its 1,000,000 population surrounded by a sea of 300,000,000 Mohametans in whose face it has just spat, emboldened by the brawn of its big American lackey. The lackey is still big, still stupid, still willing -- but he is 5,000 miles away, and the concern will grow graver in Israel, and in secret places there, evacuation plans are being re-examined...

A fourth inevitable development is the weakening of the American position in Japan, and within a few years it is quite possible we will see the final expulsion of the American occupation troops from Japan. Even today these troops are ordered to wear mufti on the Japanese streets, and it is unavoidable that the coming intensification of Russian policy against the Jewish American regime of Washington will automatically heighten the nationalist activity of the politically-conscious Japanese elite.

Many other developments *must* follow, developments which no head in the Kremlin is now contemplating. Some are regular, and foreseeable, others are Imponderables and cannot even be imagined: one thing is sure -- whoever declares war on the Jew will soon be engaged in a fight of world-wide dimensions and increasing viciousness, for the power of the Jewish State-Nation-People-Race is widespread, and the leadership of this State-Nation-People-Race conducts its policy with its emotions rather than intellectually, subject as it is to obsessions and *idées fixes*.

To us in Europe, the trials are welcome; they clear the air. The opponents have now defined themselves. America recedes now to its proper position, that of the armourer and the technician, the world's assembly line, the supplier of biological units called G.I.'s to whoever is situated to pull the appropriate strings -- in the First World War, it was England, in the Second it was Jewry. As far as Europe is concerned, the Jewish leaders may as well pull down the Stars and Stripes and run up the Star of David.

It was fatuous enough to ask Europe to fight for America, it was silly enough to ask it to "defend itself against Bolshevism" -- under the leadership of Frankfurter, Lehmann, and Morgenthau -- but now it is too absurd to ask Europe to fight to wipe out "anti-semitism" in Russia. Is there one European -- just one -- who would respond to this war-aim? But today, openly, without any possible disguise, this is the *raison d'être* of the coalition against Russia, for Russia has named its chief enemy, its sole enemy, and the sly peasant leadership of pan-Slavs in the Kremlin is not given to frivolity in its foreign policy.

The trials have made easier the task of the European Liberation Front. This Front was the first organ to warn Europe of the extinction in slavery promised for it by an alliance, supposedly with America, but actually with the Culture-State-Nation-People-Race of the Jew.

We repeat our message to Europe: no European must ever fight except for sovereign Europe; no European must ever fight one enemy of Europe on behalf of another enemy.

Europe has one aim: to actualize its Destiny. This means, to reconquer its sovereignty, to reassert its mission, to establish its Imperium, to give to the world an era of order and European peace. In the actualization of this mighty, irresistible Destiny, all extraneous events are mere material to be utilized. Inwardly, therefore, the words of the London Proclamation are as true today as they were in 1948, as they will be in 1960; "No, Europe is no more interested in this projected war than in a struggle between two negro tribes in the Sudan."

THE ENEMY OF EUROPE
By *Francis Parker Yockey*

FRANCIS PARKER YOCKEY
At about the time he began his work on *The Enemy of Europe*

Forward: *Francis Yockey completed IMPERUIM in 1948. He wrote "The Enemy of Europe" in 1953 as a sequel to touch on subjects not addressed in IMPERUIM and add comments on events that had taken places since 1948. "The Enemy of Europe" was originally published in German and the Jewish regime ordered all copies to be destroyed. Only a hand full made it out of Europe.*

INTRODUCTORY NOTE

These thoughts were intended to form part of my book IMPERIUM, but for personal reasons that was not possible. They owe their present incarnation to the fact that many of those to whom that work was really addressed were unable to draw offhand the necessary conclusions. In this treatise, as in IMPERIUM, there is nothing personal, and thus, here as there, I refrain from entering the debate over political tactics. Such matters are better discussed orally.

Organic Laws constitute the vernacular of Politics. With IMPERIUM, my aim was to present those laws so that everybody who somehow identified his personal destiny, as it were, with the Destiny of Europe could draw his own conclusions from the basic principles and select his own tactics. Some people misunderstood this possibility to such an extent that they regarded the presentation of these Organic Laws as just another contribution to the usual politico-theoretical discussion. Therefore the Organic Laws are more fully elaborated here in that they are applied to the world situation of the moment, to help provide the worthiest minds with a clearer insight into it and to unmask the Enemy of Europe.

Politics, History, Life, and Destiny heed no system. Yet if Europeans would take an active part in the world power-struggle, now, more than ever before, they must put their politics on an intellectual basis, for no physical force whatever is available to them. They must outwit the enemy at every turn, outplay him, until, years later, they will eventually be in a position to dictate conditions and compel fulfillment of them. The Organic Laws are presented here in the form of an intellectual exercise from which may be evolved a method of evaluating events, possibilities, decisions. A grammar that proves inadequate can be revised, but every branch of thought advances only when it has a grammar at its disposal.

This treatise was written from beginning to end in the year 1948. Only two passages, on Japan and on Russia, have undergone revision. The latter of the two, as can be readily perceived, was modified when in the past year, 1952, Russia gave its politics a new orientation. Both passages contain not a word that IMPERIUM, composed in 1947, does not also contain. Each day it is reconfirmed that Japan emerged from the Second World War victorious, as was noted in IMPERIUM. Russia's break with Jewry marks the beginning of the end of Bolshevism. It is called forth by the true, religious Russia, which abhors politics and technics, and which has been dominated by Petrinism and Moscovite Bolshevism alike. Of course, this break was only a beginning, but the final, inner collapse of Bolshevism is unavoidable. The possibility-indeed, I must say, the inevitability-of the destruction of Bolshevism by the true Russia is posited in IMPERIUM.

The Enemy of Europe is complete in itself, and its thesis in regard to the nature of America is true without qualification. Having lived for several decades in America, I have seen with my own eyes the distorted development of that country since the Revolution of 1933. For the most part, the resistance to the progressive distortion of America is merely passive-the resistance which any material whatever opposes to that which is acting upon it. Where the resistance is active-and the dimensions of such resistance are scanty-it finds little support, since idealism and heroism do not flourish in an atmosphere wherein economics is the ruling spirit.

Europe can attach no hopes to this resistance in America. For practical political purposes, the "White America" which still existed in its strength in the 1920's has today ceased to exist. Whether that submerged spirit will rise again in some remote future is unforeseeable. In any case, Europe cannot allow itself the luxury of dreaming that a revolution in America by the pro-European elements will lead to Europe's Liberation.

Europeans are familiar with America's propaganda for export, but less familiar with its internal propaganda. This propaganda utterly dwarfs, in its scale as well as its effect, anything Europeans can readily imagine. The Washington regime's leading internal thesis-which has not changed since 1933-is that Americans must be "tolerant" of the alien elements (which now number roughly 50% of the population), since, after all, these aliens are "brothers." "Brotherhood" is glorified on all public occasions, by all public officials, is taught in the schools and preached in the churches, which have been coordinated into the master-plan of the Culturally-alien Washington regime. Newspapers, books, magazines, radio, television, films-all vomit forth the same "Brotherhood." The "Brotherhood" propaganda is a ghastly caricature of the Christian idea of the Fatherhood of God and the Brotherhood of Man, but there is no religious intent to the propaganda. Its sole purpose is to destroy whatever exclusiveness, national feelings, or racial instincts may still remain in the American population after twenty years of national leprosy. The result of the "tolerance" and "brotherhood" campaign is that the alien enjoys a superior position in America-he can demand to be "tolerated." The American can demand nothing. The tragic fact is that the attenuation of the national instincts has proceeded so far that one cannot envisage how a Nationalist Revolution would be even possible in America.

So long as America was dominated by men of stocks from Culture-European soil, America was a European colony, even though sometimes vocally rebellious. But the America that has been distorted by the Revolution of 1933 is lost to Europe. Let no European dream of help or cooperation from that quarter.

What has occurred in the world since the publication of IMPERIUM, how the inner development of Europe has progressed, makes it clearer than ever that the world-outlook and heroic ethic manifested here are the only thing that yet offers Europe a hope of fulfilling its mighty Destiny.

THE FIRST INTERBELLUM-PERIOD 1919-1930

All wars are in some way related to politics, and the aim of Politics is to obtain power. If a state emerges from a war with less power at its disposal than it had at the beginning of the war, then it has lost the war. Whose troops return from the battlefield and whose troops lie dead on it does not matter: military victory may involve real, political victory, or it may not. Incidents outside the military arena can transform a mere military victory into an actual political defeat.

Thus it happened that the chief losers in the First World War were England and Germany. The chief victor was Japan; it won no military victory, of course, for the simple reason that it had not actively participated in the conflict. Russia, directly after its revolutionary transformation, found itself in a position that gave it an enormous increase of power, since Germany and the Austro-Hungarian Empire had been eliminated as European Great Powers. America was a political victor, but, lacking political experience and a leader-stratum, it was completely unable to consolidate its new power-position; hence it had to abandon most of its winnings.

Germany's losses are obvious: loss of twenty percent of its territory, complete loss of its foreign credits and its colonial empire, loss of the greater part of its rolling stock and its mineral wealth, loss of its prestige-it was robbed of everything under the Versailles dictate.

But England had to resign itself to even greater losses. To America it completely lost its influence in the Western Hemisphere and, just as completely, its former supremacy at sea; to Russia it had to surrender its position in Central Asia; to Japan and America its power-position in the Pacific; and to the colored world-revolution its international prestige.

The War undermined the British Empire, and more particularly, it thoroughly undermined the British Raj. Led by revolutionaries like Gandhi, the subject peoples of India began to take matters into their own hands. Soon the White rulers discovered that their voice had lost its authority. They saw themselves forced to negotiate at every moment with the active, awakened, native population, and, both personally and officially, they had to learn to behave with great circumspection. Similar things occurred among the subjugated peoples of Europe's other colonial powers. Everywhere in the Colored World the White European lost power and prestige. In this manner, not only did the two leading European states, England and Germany, lose the War, but so did the entire Western Culture, although that organism, *in toto*, had not participated militarily in it. Neutral Holland thus suffered a political defeat in the War, proving once again that political defeat does not depend on military defeat.

In the case of France, political and military victory coincided. Before the War, France was the weakest of the Great Powers; in the 1920's, it was the master of Europe. Indeed, it felt itself able once more to play the role of Napoleon, the opposition vis-à-vis England, and during the transitory political hegemony of France over continental Europe the diplomatic struggle between France and England was the most dynamic on earth.

Within the political world, power is constantly in motion. There are strong but shallow currents of power which can temporarily work against the deeper, truer, farther-aiming power-currents. France was, in regard to its military, industrial and natural resources, to all appearances absolutely secure in Europe for the immediate future. In 1923, ignoring England's protests, it undertook a military invasion of Germany. At that time, two German thinkers were discussing the European situation. When the one expressed his opinion that within a decade Germany would again be the centre-of gravity in European politics, the other, who was a "realist," rudely broke off the conversation. Hermann Keyserling was "realist" enough to recognize "reality"-any banker's apprentice can do that-, but Spengler was thinking of the source of power in Europe, of the Destiny of the Western Civilization.

During the 1930's, French mastery over Europe dwindled away like a morning mist. There was no great crisis at that time, no epochal war. The very fact of the European Revolution of 1933 dissolved French hegemony without a struggle, without a trace of hostilities. France's position was due solely to material factors, to simple control of the apparatus of power. The inner qualities of the regime that had this power at its disposal were not equal to asserting and preserving it. This regime was the bearer of no World-Hypothesis, no Idea, no Ethic. Its dynamism was a crude desire for mastery: it utterly lacked the feeling of a super-personal Mission, lacked a world-outlook, a European Hypothesis. When it was confronted with the European Revolution of 1933, its power simply evaporated. Bayonets can give one neither a good conscience nor the Inner Imperative to rule. The vassals defected, and France suddenly found itself in the position of a vassal vis-à-vis England. The choice of its lord and master was the last formal act testifying to the political existence of France as a nation.

A nation is simply an Idea, not a mass of people, not even the form into which that mass has been shaped. This form is the expression of the Idea, and the Idea is primary. Before the Idea there is no nation; when the Idea has fulfilled itself, the nation has disappeared for ever. It matters not whether custom, form, nomenclature, diplomacy, and the material apparatus of power remain to convince yesterday romantics that the nation survives. The Holy Roman Empire survived as a form until 1806, but as a political fact it had ceased to exist with the decay of the power of the Hohenstaufens after the battle at Legnano in 1176. However, in Politics, facts, not claims, not names, nor legalistic fictions are normative. In religious times, in an age of faith, men may again use in the realm of Politics words that have long ceased to describe facts. But in this Age of Absolute Politics, political fictions have lost their charm for stronger minds, no less than their effectiveness.

The death of a nation is a Ponderable, an event that must come to expression, and its When can be foreseen with sufficient accuracy to be made the basis of long-range policy. A nation shows that it is dying when it ceases to believe in its Mission and its superiority. It begins to hate everything new and everything that would drive it forward. It looks about, and seeks to make defensive preparations in every direction. No longer does it strive to enlarge, but is content merely to maintain, its power-position. *To preserve power, however, one must continually increase it*. A nation need not die tumultuously in a great military defeat. As a rule, nations die quite peacefully, sinking deeper and deeper into sterile conservatism and shrinking back more and more from great decisions.

THE LIQUIDATION OF ENGLISH SOVEREIGNTY

English policy was senile already at the beginning of Joseph Chamberlain's career in government. Even his grand idea of English-German-American world-hegemony, though still a forceful, virile, aggressive policy, was basically static: behind it lay the age-old dream of bringing History finally to a close. After Chamberlain's time, English policy became completely toothless, and names like Grey, Lloyd-George, MacDonald, and Baldwin show the depths of the descent into national oblivion, when compared with names from more youthful days: Walpole, Pitt, Castlereagh, Canning, Gladstone. The great Empire Builders were eager for every large conquest; their dim successors indulged in lamentations over the status quo, expending their feeble energies on protecting it from young and virile "aggressors." These pallbearers of the Empire tried to build a wall against History by describing Politics in terms of Law: The status quo is "legal," every change therein, however, is "illegal." Political dynamism is "illegal:" Power-relationships must be continued as they were at the time of the Versailles dictate. After Versailles, England no longer had the national-political energy to increase its power; hence everybody was to be morally prohibited from doing so, and this moral coercion was codified in sacred "treaties," which were signed on the muzzles of cannon. To maintain England's political supremacy was "moral" and "legal"-respect for "international morality and the sanctity of treaties" it was called. "Observing international law," "orderly procedure in international relations," and similar political absurdities were promulgated. This was not the first time that one engaged in politics in order to put politics in legalistic wrappings. The politician who resorts to law and morality to disguise his power-position is suffering from a bad political conscience, and the politician or the state with a bad conscience is decadent. Ascendant politics is not afraid of being politics. Decadent politics passes itself off as religion, law, morality, science-in short, as anything other than Politics.

Of course, England's attempt to impose its form on the world by the simple trick of employing legalistic jargon was completely futile. Only the English population was deceived thereby, just as later with the propaganda about the invulnerability of Singapore. But on the power currents of the world, which reflect the development of super-personal organisms, the jargon had no effect whatsoever.

From the original standpoint of regarding the status quo as inviolable only insofar as the English power-position was concerned, one went on to that of regarding the status quo everywhere as sacrosanct. Thus English policy, in complete distortion of English interests, was made to support the Serbian, Romanian, and Bohemian states against the power-currents that were destined to destroy those artificial political structures.

The cost of a distorted policy must be set high. The state with a distorted policy can gain no accretion of power; thus even its military and diplomatic victories are defeats. During the third decade of the 20th century, England gradually handed over its sovereignty to America in order to continue pursuing its distorted policy, a policy devoted to the world-wide preservation of the status quo. Naturally, such an unpleasant fact was not admitted by the representatives of a certain mentality, and naturally again-those who bore the responsibility for the transfer of power shied away from defining the new relationship precisely; for had they done so, the whole policy would have been spoilt. Nevertheless, when Baldwin announced in 1936 that he would not deploy the English fleet without consulting America beforehand, he informed the entire political world in unmistakable terms that the end of English independence had come, that English sovereignty had passed over to America. Independence means being able to act alone. Sovereignty means being answerable to nobody except oneself. Neither Independence nor Sovereignty was characteristic of the English government that started the Second World War with its declaration of war on Germany in September, 1939.

When a nation loses its sovereignty, any foreign peoples and territories it controls pass, of organic necessity, into the sphere of influence of powers that are sovereign. Thus Denmark, for example, as a result of the Second World War, was absorbed into the American world-system. This occurred quite automatically; it was simply a process of the Organic law of the Political Plenum, which ordains that a power-vacuum in the political world is impossibility.

A state is not to be regarded as a power unless it can make decisions alone. Units like Switzerland are artificial structures whose raison d'être is to serve as buffers for the adjacent powers, and thus owe their existence to the mutual jealousy of those powers. They are anomalies that can exist only so long as their territory has no particular strategic value for the surrounding Great Powers. During the 19th century, Switzerland was exactly the opposite of a power-vacuum. It was the point-of-convergence for the powers surrounding it and was likewise penetrated by the power-currents surrounding them. The statecraft of the Swiss "politician" consisted in abstaining from all politics and in dodging all decisions. As soon as Switzerland ceased, in 1945, to be the convergence-point for the bordering powers, that very moment it became an American vassalage, without hopes, wishes, fears, or even official recognition of its status. Throughout the 19th century, the Netherlands was only an English bridgehead on the continent, first against France (until about 1865), then against Prussia-Germany. The Netherlands had no sovereignty, and its military forces stood at England's disposal, very tactless though it would have been to speak about this in England or its protectorate.

The simple, terrifying truth is that, through the diplomacy of its leaders, beginning with Lloyd George, England lost its independence, parted with its established mode of political conduct, and passed into the same vassal-like relation vis-à-vis America into which, say, Holland or Norway had passed vis-à-vis England in the 19th century. It is utterly pointless to connect the national demise of England with the complete fecklessness of parliamentary government in the Age of Absolute Politics, to attempt to construct a causal relationship out of it.

For nations have a certain time-span before them, and their political phase also has an organically predetermined rhythmic course. Material factors have nothing to do with the greater movements of the power-currents within the political world. The merely ephemeral supremacy of France in the 1920's, based solely upon material factors, is the best example of this in recent times.

ORIGINS OF THE WAR

To understand the origins and the morphology of the Second World War, it is necessary to grasp the fact that England passed into the American sphere of influence not after, but before, the War. In 1942, a member of Parliament stated that it appeared to him as though England had the choice of becoming an eastern outpost of America or a Western outpost of Germany. His statement did not cover all the possibilities, and was imprecise, but it was at least based on the political fact that England's independence and sovereignty had ceased to exist.

English independence began to dwindle away from the moment in History when English policy sought to preserve rather than to enlarge the overseas Empire. Inwardly, this point was reached when England's Conservatism, which had formerly meant respect for the Past, shifted to hostility towards the Future. The establishment of American hegemony over the Island could be proved by citing documents, diplomatic agreements, overseas telephone conversations, and the like. But such things, indispensable as they are to the historian, the journalist, and the armchair politician, are all quite unimportant from a larger point of view. For the great, indisputable facts of politics themselves show sufficiently the underlying power-currents. Neither power nor its movements can be concealed. What are those facts?

The aim of Politics is to obtain power. As we have seen, an elderly organism aims expressly at maintaining the present circumference of its power, although the precondition for maintaining power is the acquisition of more power. From the actual nature of Politics (and accordingly one could also say, from the nature of super-personal organisms and the human beings in their service), it is evident that a political unit must not recklessly enter upon a war that cannot increase its power. To the entire world it was obvious that England could not have increased its power through a war against Germany.

A war that a political unit is not capable of pushing through to victory on its own cannot increase the power of that unit. The term "political unit" is used here in the strict sense, of course, and means a unit that possesses true sovereignty and thus has the ability to decide on its own initiative the War-Peace question; therefore this term cannot be applied to areas like Brazil and Canada. If allies are indispensable-not merely practicable and useful-for bringing the war to a victorious conclusion, then these allies will be the real power-beneficiaries of a successful war. The term "allies" describes only other, real political, units which can make the War-Peace decision on their own initiative; and here, too, areas like Colombia and South Africa are excluded. Obviously, not even with the remnants of its Empire and with its dependencies, France and Poland, could England have defeated Germany. It must be assumed that what was known to the entire world was also known to official circles in London. Nevertheless, in September, 1939, England began a war against Germany.

After the American declaration of war in December, 1941, it was officially admitted in England that the primary goal of pre-war English diplomacy had consisted in winning American military aid. What was not admitted, but was just as notoriously certain at the time, was that England's war-declaration had been made, first, with complete and unlimited confidence in America's assistance in every form; second, to carry out a policy that had been set in Washington and that in no way meant the continuance of English national policy.

It does not matter who begot the miscarriage called "collective security" a mixture of legalism, naïveté, stupidity, envy, and senility. The fact is certain that only two powers in the world benefited from this policy: Russia and America. The government in London did not willingly favor Russia, but it worked, with full awareness of what it was doing, under pressure from the Washington regime, exactly according to its instructions.

The salient point here is that this fact, although satisfactorily proved by war memoirs, confessions, documents, and such, is manifest in the great decisions themselves. By way of example: If a power enters a war that it cannot win militarily, and that would not cause any power to accrue to it even if it did win a military victory, it requires no searching through history books to know that "power" is not acting in its own interests. In other words, it is a protectorate. From the standpoint of the Washington regime, the remnants of the English State were useful as a means of entangling America in a war against Germany, according to the 1916 formula, and the English Island was valuable as an "unsinkable aircraft carrier" - in the words of the American General Staff-, likewise as a conduit for men and materiel.

In these events, the relationship of England to America did not differ essentially from that of, say, Poland or Serbia. The Washington regime had England just as much at its disposal as it did Poland and Serbia. Only the strong power in a coalition can be said to have allies;

the others merely are allies. In 1948, the post-War French government officially appealed to America as the "ally of France." This appeal requires no explanation. History consists of the ridiculous as well as the sublime.

A state that needs allies can never obtain them; it can become the ally of another, more powerful state, and fight for the increase of that power, but the state that needs to ally is the subordinate one. An alliance is never the sentimental grouping of a club, dripping with friendship that the journalists want to make it out to be. On the contrary, every alliance has as its basis Protection and Obedience. Taken strictly, Washington and Moscow had no alliance during the Second World War, since the relationship showed obedience, to be sure, on the part of the Washington regime without protection (which is a corollary of authority) on the part of Russia. In a Protection-Obedience relationship, the protectorate is within the sphere of influence of the Protector, and therefore must obey it. However, America's self-robbery on behalf of the Russian war-effort was thoroughly voluntary, even though it was in complete opposition to America's national interests.

Two degrees of political stupidity are to be found in diplomacy. The first is short-range: lack of political skill, inability to carry on any negotiations successfully and to recognize short-term advantages. The second is long-range: lack of political far-sightedness, ignorance of deeper power-currents and the Ponderables of the Becoming. These two kinds of political stupidity stand in the same relation to each other as the Military stands to the Political. The Military is the weapon and the servant of the Political. Only disaster can come of military thought dominating political thought. "Win the War!" can never be an expression of Politics, for Politics is concerned with identifying the power-currents, choosing the Enemy, and weighing in relation to the national interest all happenings, inner and outer, according to how the war develops. To elevate the slogan "Win the War!" to the rank of policy, as America did during the Second World War, is the equivalent of saying that there is nothing political about the war. Military thought is simply not political thought. The permanent ambition of all military thought is to win a military victory; the corresponding ambition of all political thought is to win more power. That may or may not be implicit in a policy that seems to desire military victory at whatever cost, for one can probably adduce just as many historical examples of political and military victory occurring separately as of both coinciding neutrally. Likewise, if short-range political thinking constantly prevails over the long-range in the policy decisions of a state, the only possible result is that state's political extinction. No matter how skillfully executed its political maneuvers, if a state has ignored the larger power-currents in puzzling out its policy, it will suffer a political defeat.

All these explanations and definitions apply only to real political units, for the microscopic destinies of such dwarfish "states" as San Marino, Monaco, and Belgium are completely determined by the Destinies of the true political units, the Great Powers, as the diplomatic concert of the 19th century liked to call them.

The Polish officials of 1939 were politically stupid in the first sense. Their country encircled by two Great Powers that had just concluded a non-aggression pact, they nonetheless chose to enter upon a war that would mean for it direct, permanent political extinction in the least desirable form: occupation and partition. Actually, it is pure charity to call the political dealings of those officials stupidity instead of treason, for shortly after the beginning of the War, they disappeared, going abroad to live on the capital they were able to amass owing to their policy. Treason and political stupidity are closely related to each other. In The Proclamation of London it is stated: "Treason is nothing but incapacity when it becomes resolute." As used here, the word "treason" refers to treasonous conduct on the part of individuals. An individual may be able to better his personal-economic circumstances through an act of treason, but no group, no class, no organic stratum within a country is ever able to better the power-position of the country through a large-scale act of treason. In this sense, all treason is political stupidity.

The English officials of 1939 were politically stupid in the second sense in that they completely failed to identify the larger power-currents and likewise totally lacked statesmanlike feeling for the Definition of Enemy: The Enemy is the state that one can defeat and thereby gain more power. Thus military victory over an opponent whose defeat proves so costly that one must take in the bargain a greater loss of power elsewhere must be called political defeat.

These English officials approached diplomatic preparations for the Second World War according to the old tried and true methods. They attempted to isolate Germany, concluding wherever possible war-alliances with Germany's neighbors (the "Peace Front"). They counted on American aid, trusting in the Washington regime's assurances that it would be able to lead America to war-despite the geopolitical position of America, despite the unanimous opposition of the American people, despite the conflict between intervention and the national interests of America, and finally, despite the fundamental spiritual indifference of Americans towards even a victorious war against Europe.

The question they failed to ask was: What is the final political aim? Or in other words: How will England's power be increased through a victorious American war against Germany? Had they asked this question, it would have been obvious to them that, since England could not win this war alone, any extension of power derived from a defeat of Germany would be for the benefit of America, or some other power. The result of their failure to ask this question was England's total defeat.

The suicide-policy of the English regime in 1939-it was continued throughout the War-has various roots, and the ultimate explanation of it will keep scholars and archivists busy. The essential facts are already well-known. First, political stupidity alone is not to blame: Some members of the government consciously and deliberately pursued a policy that was not pro-English, only anti-German. Second, some members of this regime were not officially part of the government, indeed, not even part of the English organism. Third, and most importantly, with Joseph Chamberlain the rich political tradition of England had been laid to rest. The succeeding statesmen were of lesser caliber; class-warriors, like Lloyd George and MacDonald; pure egotists, capable of representing any alien interest, like Churchill and Eden; even obsessed psychopaths, like Duff Cooper.

Thomas Hardy did well to introduce the Spirit of Irony into his Napoleonic drama, The Dynasts, in which the paradoxical and the ironic make up the favorite conversation of Clio. How ridiculous in retrospect now seem the efforts of those officials in London during the period from 1939 to 1941: They sought to drag America into the War! In reality, the War was from beginning to end a creation of the Washington regime. If it ended in victory, victory could mean only an increase in power for that regime, or some other political unit, but in no case for England. The English nation was impressed into the War as a vassal that had been made to believe it was acting independently, and it emerged from the War with every characteristic of a colony. Only the definitive, legalistic formulation was wanting. Those at the head of the London regime who were honest, if also stupid, schemed to use America for their purposes. And precisely because of their scheming, they were used to forward the ambitions of the Washington regime.

STRONGER POWER-CURRENTS
IN THE AGE OF ABSOLUTE POLITICS

Before the First World War, the most comprehensive single power current in the world was the movement of power out of Europe to the colonial areas-to America, to the Far East, to the Near East, to

Africa. Power is spiritual in origin. That can mean only that Europe, seen from without, from Asia, Africa, and the Americas-was in spiritual decline. England was the nation that was then custodian of the Destiny of Europe. Other European powers had far-flung possessions and interests in the world, but none other than England could boast of a World Empire. To the outer world England was the West. However, the English national Idea had been completely fulfilled in the course of the 19th century; the English nation, as distinct from the English People, was too used up and too worn out to bear the burden of the Destiny of Europe. This fact could not be concealed, and so the scales of power between the West and the Outer Forces tipped over more in favor of the Outer Forces.

Thus it was England's political weakness that ignited the Asiatic masses' anti-European will-to-annihilation. In 1900, the English Empire, including the seas on which England was indisputably supreme, covered 17/20ths of the surface of the earth. To maintain this structure in that form the entire political strength of Europe would have been needed. Joseph Chamberlain's project of an Anglo-German partnership was based upon this insight. Other political minds that had the art of empathizing correctly apprehended the power-current at the time, and the whole world was familiar with the expression Kaiser Wilhelm II coined for these stirrings: The Yellow Peril. The great fact of the "Yellow Peril" dominated the political world-picture before the First World War.

Within Europe, the great power-current went from England to Germany. The lesser powers France and Austria were both in the process of dissolution, and both passed into vassalage: Austria to Germany, France to England. But already England had entered the organically inevitable stage in which power moves according to the laws of centrifugal force. Power-currents moved from England to the strongest outlying powers, to Russia in Central Asia, to Japan in China and the Pacific, and to America in the Western Hemisphere. To Germany, Japan, and America, England gradually lost its position in world commerce, and on the seas it had to yield to the same three political units.

The metapolitical explanation for the intra-European power-current from England to Germany is simple. The decline and inevitable demise of the English Nation-Idea was part of the development of the Western Culture from the first phase of Civilization, the Age of Economics, to the second phase, the Age of Absolute Politics. It was Destiny that England, the nation with the state-less articulation, to which the Ideas of predestination and laissez-faire had been given, to which they were instinctive, to which expansion meant a business-like plundering of the conquered territory with as little political disintegration in it as possible, was the guardian of the Western Civilization during the 19th century. Likewise it was Destiny, and not chance, that the coming to an end of that age of liberalism, parliamentarism, economics, laissez-faire, and trade-imperialism also meant the coming to an end of England's power. The new age, the Age of Absolute Politics, in which Politics rules unconditionally over every aspect of life in the Western Civilization, demands a different type of nation, a different International, a different Universal-Hypothesis to fulfill the Cultural Mission of the 20th century and the centuries to come. The Prussian-German nation is that one of the Western nations whose national Idea thoroughly corresponds to the Cultural Imperative in this Age of Absolute Politics. For the solution of its tasks this Age demands the old Roman virtues: a soldierly ethos and honor-feeling, political-organisatory talent, firmness, conscientiousness, devotion to duty, will-to-power instead of will-to-plunder. Since the Prussian Idea agrees with the Spirit of the Age, power flows organically, naturally, irresistibly to the focus of this Idea.

That a general war would break out, all statesmen and political thinkers were agreed; only its form was not foreseen, nor could it have been. The natural form corresponding to the power-problems posed by the power currents-would have been England and Germany versus Russia and Japan. Since England and Germany belonged to the same Culture and had a common Destiny, as they always shall, any war between these two states had to benefit powers outside Europe to so great an extent that neither one of them could have profited from it, and that quite independent of which won a military victory and which suffered a military defeat. Therefore, it was in the interest of each of the two, for its own wellbeing no less than that of the Western Culture, to undertake power struggles only against extra-European forces.

After the War erupted into a false form, viz., into a form that in no way corresponded to the power-problems posed by the power-currents, the outward movement of power from Europe vastly accelerated. The European Raj in India was undermined; Japan was freed from all fetters to Europe, and left with America as its sole power-rival. America became the ruling power at sea, despite the Five-Power-Naval Treaty of 1921, under which it scuttled 750,000 tons of new shipping. That folly hardly changed anything, simply because of America's increased ability to build ships, which may be ascribed to the War, and because of the powerful spiritual impetus of the War, because of America's awakening from its century of isolation, an isolation comparable to that of a silkworm in its cocoon. After the

Bolshevist Revolution of 1917 and the consolidation of the Asiatic Moscow regime, Russia entered the political world as its most secure power. In Europe, France inherited the continental hegemony that England had striven to take from Germany.

Germany lost power, true; however England lost even more. It shared in a local, military victory as part of a world-coalition and paid for it with a general, political defeat. With results, England had applied the great fundamental of strategy precisely in reverse: it employed all its strength on inconsequential points while reserving as little of it as possible for the decisive point. Vis-a-vis the Colored-Asiatic world, England was still the custodian of the Destiny of Europe, to be sure, now more enfeebled than ever, a pale shadow of the Imperialist England at the time of the Silver Jubilee of 1887. England no longer had the feeling of a Mission, no longer felt itself called upon to rule- one no longer spoke of an Empire, but of "Mandates"-, it no longer believed in itself. Even domestically England was in moral and material chaos. The War had resulted in the New Age, with its new values, and the discarding of much that was formerly significant, and the old Idea of parliamentarism and laissez-faire was ineffectual in this bewildering new state of affairs. A super-personal Idea that has fulfilled itself can evolve no further. In a healthy, organic evolution, England would have adopted the new super-personal Idea, the new Hypothesis, and been absorbed into the new International, but the catastrophic form of the First World War prevented the normal evolution. The West was not represented before the world by a powerful, firm alliance of England and Germany, militarily and politically victorious over Russia and Japan, but by a superannuated English Capitalism.

Had the War assumed the organic form, an English-German coalition against the rising Asiatic menace, it would have ended in a European victory and brought the whole planet under the influence of Europe. But in the form events took, the West lost so much of the 17/20ths of the surface of the earth it had controlled that only about 4/20ths remained subject to it. And so the two great power-currents continued unabated, the centrifugal current from Europe to the Outer Forces and the centripetal current from England to Germany.

Power in embryonic spiritual form streamed from England to Germany. All Europe looked increasingly to the Prussian Ethos for guidance. This idea gained irresistibly in moral force, strength of its Inner Imperative, and Cultural prestige. Within Europe, another, lesser power-current flowed, from France to Italy, this time actual political power. The source of this current was the Genius of a single man, Mussolini. He effected the transformation of Italy by infusing it with the Prussian-German Socialist Ethos. Since the petty-nationalism of the 19th century had not yet been overcome in Italy, as elsewhere, Mussolini was forced to associate his new State-building Ethos with the name of Imperial Rome. Italy and the entire Western Civilization have no inward connection with Imperial Rome, nor did it stand in any relation to them. Therefore, it may not be amiss if the true inspiration of his Genius is mentioned here. Mussolini himself designated Nietzsche and Sorel as the two teachers who had inspired him. Both were opponents of laissez-faire, both were anti-parliamentary, anti-liberal, anti-democratic; both had strong authoritarian leanings.

The centrifugal power-current from Europe outwards flowed more strongly to Japan, Russia, and America. Weak heads in England looked disconsolately to the American colony, symbolized in its spiritual endowments by its politically moronic leaders, like Wilson, Lansing, and Harding, and hoped for spiritual leadership and material support from it. That kept on even after Americans demonstrated loudly and clearly that they were quite indifferent to European politics, as their Congress showed when it refused to ratify the Treaty of Versailles and thereby rejected membership for America in the League of Nations. In consequence of the longing for American domination on the part of a certain group of Europeans-especially numerous and influential on the Island-, the totally altered American leadership that resulted from the American Revolution of 1933 found an open road to the financial-diplomatic conquest of France, England, and the Netherlands. Thenceforth America intervened in all intra-European affairs, always with the intention of promoting the same negative policy, meaning "collective security," which can be called both anti-German and pro-Bolshevist.

Here are outlined the epochal events of the Interbellum Period **1919-1939:**

1919 Versailles dictate; French hegemony established in Europe. Spengler's work Preussentum and Sozialismus appears.

1921 Mussolini emerges in History; the first open revolt in Europe of Socialism against Capitalism, of Authority against Money, of Faith against Criticism, of Discipline against Laissez-faire, of Duty-Consciousness against the ideology of "happiness," of Hierarchy against Equality, of the Will-to-Power against the Will-to-Plunder.

1923 France invades Germany; high point of France's power in its domination of continental Europe.

1931 Collapse of the international financial structure of Capitalism; economic catastrophe resulting there from; economic depression throughout the Western Civilization. Japan successfully raises its claim to power-monopoly in the Far East with its annexation of Manchuria.

1933 On 30th January: The **European Revolution**. Revolt of the Spirit of Authority against Money, of Socialism against Capitalism; overthrow of the 1918 pseudo-victory of Capitalism. The **American Revolution of 1933**. Assumption of power by the Jewish entity. Lasting transformation of American policy through abandonment of nationalistic isolationism and the introduction of an internationalist policy. Formation of the Jewish-American Symbiosis begins. End of French hegemony over Europe.

1936 Four-Power Pact: England, France, Germany, and Italy forever renounce waging war among themselves; the first collective attempt to form an organically determined European Imperium.

August-September: America successfully intervenes to prevent the ratification of the Four-Power Pact, to abort the European Imperium and to make possible a second World War-this in order to destroy the power of Europe and to forestall the rise throughout the world of Authoritarian Socialism to the detriment of Finance Capitalism. This is the year in which the English Prime Minister Baldwin made his statement about the dependence of England and France on America.

1938 Munich Agreement for the pacification of Europe. The Four Powers act together to end Czech domination over Germans, Slovaks, Hungarians, and Ruthenians. Last of the great European efforts to overcome petty-statism and to establish a provisional European Imperium without an intra-European war. American meddling in England succeeds in annulling the mutual English- German renunciation of war and forces a reorientation of English policy towards setting up a warfront against Germany.

1939 Formation of the "peace front," a war-alliance of the Americanized England against Germany as diplomatic preparation for the Second World War.

September: Final success of the American policy. Outbreak of the

English War against Socialism and the Reawakening of Authority.

1941 Attack on Russia by the provisional European Imperium. The War gains a second aspect.

November: The Washington regime presents its war-ultimatum to Japan as a means of provoking a Japanese attack that would facilitate the intervention of America in the European War against the wishes of the American populace.

December: Japan responds militarily to the ultimatum, whereby the Washington regime knows in advance the time and place of the attack. Complete destruction of the American fleet at Pearl Harbor by Japan- this because the Washington regime deliberately delays every defensive measure. America declares war on Europe; Europe becomes the chief enemy and is designated the main front The War expands into and shows itself from a third aspect.

THE THREE ASPECTS OF THE WAR

In this Age of Absolute Politics, Culture provides the motivation for Great Wars. From 1000 to 1500 A.D., the inner-Politics of Europe was determined by fealty. The motivation for the intra-European power-struggles during the centuries up to the Congress of Vienna was religious and dynastic; during the 19th century, it was nationalistic and economic. After 1900, the whole planet became increasingly active politically. The decline of England's power awakened in the Colored World the illusion that the entire Western Culture found itself in a state of decreasing power. That was false indeed, but the outbreak of the First World War and the world-wide verdict against Western Power and Western prestige seemed to confirm this misconception, Since the scale of political activity has become planetary, only two spiritual possibilities for a conflict remain: first, the Western Idea of world-rule (and for over two centuries, directly or indirectly, the West actually did rule the greater part of the world); and, second, the Outer Revolt, which is simply the negation of this Western Idea. Manifestations of the Western world-empire Idea were: the British Empire, and all other European overseas-empires; the Americans' conquest of their continent, American imperialism in the Pacific; Germany's enduring desire for expansion into the Slavic areas and its pushing back of the eastern frontier of the Western Culture during the millennium 1000-2000. Manifestations of the Outer Revolt were: the Chinese Opium War against England; the Indian Mutinies of 1857 and 1947; the Zulu Wars; the Mexican revolt against

Maximilian, the Mexican revolution of 1910; the Chinese revolution of 1911; the Philippine insurrections against Spain and the latter Philippine uprisings against America, 1900-1946; the Bolshevist Revolution of 1917; the Japanese War Against the West, 1941-1945.

Thus the power-front is seen to be based on Culture as the dominant spiritual front in world politics, and all other politics, be it primitive, local, or personal, is overshadowed by this tremendous disjunction. On the planet there is only one High Culture in the process of fulfillment, the Western Culture. Outside that Culture, there are only remnants of dead Cultures, whose peoples have once again become primitive, fellaheen, like the Chinese, Hindu, and Islamic; savages, like the African and American aborigines; barbarians, like the Russians and certain tribes in Central Asia. All peoples living outside the West have perforce taken over many Western customs and characteristics, since the uniquely powerful imperialism of the West lays claim to the whole earth, and its performance has forced the people of the world to acknowledge the undeniable intellectual and material superiority of Europe. This does not mean, however, that "Westernization" can ever be anything other than superficial. When the Western Culture says "Yes" to its Imperialistic urge, it naturally calls forth a reaction among those who do not belong to it. Their organic response is an equally passionate "No". When they take up Western methods, it is only to use them against the West: If spears cannot defeat Whites, let us learn how to build factories and produce machines!

From a Cultural standpoint, the Second World War consisted of three organically separable wars. The first of these was an intra-Cultural war: England versus Germany. In the terminology of Ideas, it was a war of Capitalism versus Socialism. But as these two great outlooks have an organic relation to each other, it was actually a struggle between the Past and the Future, for Capitalism belongs to the Past, Authoritarian Ethical Socialism to the Future. Since the Past can never overcome the fact of the Future, except in semblance, this intra-Cultural war had only two possible results: Victory of the Idea of Ethical Socialism or Chaos within the entire Western organism.

The second of these wars began with the attack by the provisional European Imperium on Russia, the leader of the Outer Revolt against Western world-rule. The natural, organic form of this war would have been Europe with all its colonies-America, South Africa, Australia, Argentina, et al.-against Russia and the other Asiatic powers. Thus it would have ended in the political destruction of the Asiatic powers, including Russia, and in the establishment of Western world-rule in a stricter, more absolute form than the Western Empire, let us say, of 1900.

The third of these wars was related to the second: the American war against Japan, like the European war against Russia, was a war of the West against the Outer Revolt. In this war, America's role was that of a Western colony, and its victory over Japan was also a victory for Europe, just as a victory of Europe over Russia would have been a victory also for America.

The first, the intra-European war, very quickly lost the character of such, since England's total war-effort was brought ever more under the direction of the Washington regime, and England, likewise its remaining overseas possessions, was occupied by American troops. Thereby the Washington regime wanted to ensure that England would not attempt to bail out of the War. With the American occupation of England and the remnants of its Empire, the intra-European war of England versus Germany ended. From then on, there were two organically dissociated wars: Europe versus the American-Russian coalition and Japan versus America. Wherever the English military forces fought on, it was only for the extension of Russian or American power, for now there was no longer an English political unit whose power could be extended by a victory.

Thus America became involved in all three organically dissociated wars. Its participation in the Second World War was a struggle for the victory of the West, in regard to Japan, and simultaneously for the defeat of the West, in regard to Russia. America fought for an Asiatic victory and against an Asiatic victory.

The outcome of the second organically dissociated war, that of the European Imperium versus Russia, was complicated by America's policy vis-à-vis Russia. At the beginning of the War, Russia was prepared to conclude peace with Europe, but the Washington regime, in accordance with its purely negative, anti-American policy of defeating Authoritarian Socialist Europe at any cost, even that of national suicide, promised to give economic support to Russia's entire war-effort, so long as it would stay in the War, promised to share with it in a Russian-American world-condominium in the post-War period. America's conduct vis-à-vis Russia has never had its like in world-history. During the War, America deprived its own armed forces of huge masses of war materiel, which it delivered to Russia without charge and without any terms of repayment. America supplied Russia with: 14,795 aircraft, 7,056 tanks, 51,503 jeeps, 35,170 motorcycles, 8,071 tractors, 375,883 lorries; other machinery valued at 1,078 million dollars; 107 million yards of cotton products and 62 million yards of woolen products. (This listing is incomplete and does not include ships, foodstuffs, railway materiel, etc.) At American orders huge quantities of armaments and other vital equipment were withdrawn from the English Army and delivered to Russia, including 5,031 tanks and 6,778 aircraft. Deliveries of raw materials reached the value of 39,000,000 pounds. The American viceroy in England, Churchill, confessed in his memoirs that one of his diplomatic problems lay in persuading the Russians to accept these gifts without suspicion and with good will. Throughout the War, the Communist underground movements the whole world over received from North America weapons, munitions, explosives, clothing, medicines, foodstuffs, and financial support-this in Europe, in Serbia, and in the Far East, especially Celebes, Sumatra, Indochina, and China.

It is clear-once again from the simple Organic Laws of Politics-that the Washington regime in no way pursued an American policy. A nationalist policy can never be negative. When a nation's policy becomes negative, something has prevailed over the national interest. All during the War, American propaganda was governed by a single great imperative: Destroy Germany! In the background was the weak echo: Destroy Japan! The propaganda left no doubt, however, about the relative importance of these two negatives.

Without America's intervention as the all-sacrificing lackey of Russia, the war of Europe versus Russia could have ended in two ways: political destruction of Russia by Europe, or negotiated peace. After the American war-entry, the second possibility was eliminated. In its main aspect, the Second World War was no longer a war of Europe against Russia, but a fortiori a war of America against Europe, and this war had only one possible outcome; political destruction of Europe. The innumerable Russian troops fought practically under the same command as the troops of America and its satellites. Faced with this coalition of powers, the European Imperium had no choice but to sue for peace. The American formula of "unconditional surrender" made that impossible, however.

The third of the organically dissociated wars, Japan versus America, had three possible results: political destruction of Japan, negotiated peace, or expulsion of the American power from the Pacific. A political destruction of America was, and is, impossible, owing to America's geographic breadth and position. Only America's overseas-empire, in the Mediterranean, in Africa, in the Persian Gulf, in the Pacific, and in the Caribbean can be destroyed, not however the American political basis, autarkic and inaccessible as it is to large armies from another continent.

RESULTS OF THE WAR

After the American occupation of England, there was no longer a war between England and Germany, for the ability to wage war against an enemy of one's own choosing is the mark of a sovereign power, and England's sovereignty had ceased to exist. But there was still a spiritual-ethical "war" between the English idea of Capitalism and the Prussian-German idea of Ethical Socialism. Since, in this Age of Absolute Politics, Politics takes unto itself every aspect of Life, this spiritual-ethical conflict had to be decided by the politico-military conflict. Thus the 19th century idea of Capitalism won a pseudo-victory over the 20th century Idea of Ethical Socialism, and that meant Chaos throughout the Western Civilization. The Past cannot win an enduring victory over the Future. The later Stuarts and Bourbons learnt that, so did Metternich. It is an old lesson that must ever be learnt anew.

In its spiritual ethical aspect, the War, since it did not destroy Europe, came to its sole possible result: It weakened the Idea of Capitalism and, in the same tempo, strengthened the Idea of Socialism, by giving Socialism a victory at least in the field of Technics. After the War, the only possible way of governing and maintaining order in every Western country was through complete political regulation of economic life, in other words, through the application of Socialist techniques. Everywhere laissez-faire is dead, both nationally and internationally, except in the very highest economic sphere, that of bank and bourse. For the time being, that domain is spared state-intervention, simply because it is where the governments are chosen. Behind the parliamentary puppets stands the Master of Money.

The second war, that of the provisional European Imperium against Russia, yielded military and political victory to Russia. That politico-military victory, based on American aid, given with a largesse unique in world-history, made the Russian Empire into the world's foremost power, owing to its geopolitical position and to the poor quality of its only remaining opponent, notwithstanding that this opponent dominated a greater part of the planet than it did. England's pseudo-victory owed solely to the Washington regime's policy of sacrificing American and European interests to Russian interests. It is a fact of great importance that the Washington regime quite consciously and deliberately created the present Russian Empire as an instrument of its absolute anti-German, anti-European policy.

The third war, that of America versus Japan, was, from a Cultural standpoint, a war of Western Civilization against the Outer Revolt. To superficial observers, its outcome seemed to be political annihilation of Japan. Yet this war ended in a negotiated peace. The most important fact about Japanese history, society, and politics is that Japan contains a nation bearing stratum, a level of the population that feels itself charged with an organic Mission. America did nothing to weaken this stratum's feeling of a Mission. Through peace negotiations, the Japanese nation, state, aristocracy, and other institutions were preserved; the Japanese Army was disbanded honorably, and the Emperor, the Japanese national Idea, suffered no Oriental loss-of-face. An American army occupied the Island, and even the commander of that army spoke openly on behalf of an early termination of the occupation. This war resulted in a military and psychological victory for America, and at least for the moment, the West reasserted itself in a part of the world where it had been in retreat for 75 years. At the time, however, in IMPERIUM, I called Japan a political victor of the Second World War because its outer Mission, the expulsion of the West from Asia, had been accomplished, and its inner independence, though temporarily suspended, had not been really abolished. The Washington regime, which had but little interest in the matter of Japan, permitted its occupation forces considerable autonomy. The leaders of those forces had no idea at all of the types of power and of the over currents of power in the world. Their notion of exploiting the victory was on a journalistic plane. They regarded the main effort of the occupation not as political but as moral. In all seriousness, this leadership wanted to "educate" the Japanese nation, as though it were a child, and teach it "democracy."

The extent to which the military victory of America over Japan was also a political victory over Japan for the entire Western Civilization is thus very slight indeed. The regime's policy of reconstructing Japan undermined the greatest part of the victory. Its surrender of China and Manchuria to Russia, the leader of the Outer Revolt against Western Civilization, undermined it even further. The last remaining step, the restoration of Japanese sovereignty, is only a matter of time, for here the initiative lies with Japan. So long as the Japanese monarchy and the Japanese nation-bearing stratum, with its feeling of a Mission, survive unimpaired, a revival of Japanese sovereignty, Japanese militarism, and the Japanese Empire against America is certain.

The Outer Revolt against the West was only locally contained by America's military victory over Japan. In other parts of the Far East, the revolts were successful. The Chinese, Malays, Indonesians, and the primitive denizens of the Philippines expelled their Western masters.

In the metapolitical sense, the Western Civilization lost the War against Japan, despite the local, purely military victory of the

Americans.

THE POWER PROBLEMS OF THE WAR

The two great power-currents in the world before the Second World War were the centrifugal flow of power from the Western organism to the Outer Forces (especially away from the Continental European nations, since the obsolescence of the English national Idea led to the power current England-America), and, then, the centripetal flow of the attributes that alone make power vital and lasting, from England to Prussia-Germany.

To set forth these two power-currents as power problems - from the European standpoint -, the first problem was: How is European world hegemony to be restored? And the second was: How is Europe to be imbued with Ethical Socialism, the only viable world-outlook and nation building force in this Age of Absolute Politics?

These two problems were the actual issues of the Second World War. Men and governments cannot create power-problems; rather, these arise when super-personal organisms collide with existing power-currents. Both lie far beyond any human control. In navigating the seas, one can sail with the currents, or try to sail against them, but one cannot produce new currents. Thus it is with the Organic: The possibilities are given, and are not subject to alteration or dispute. One can either accept an organic possibility, or abandon oneself to disappointment, disease, and chaos. If a possibility is frustrated long enough, it will one day no longer be there to accept, for the Organic always has a duration of existence.

The more important of the two power-problems in determining the form of the War was the first: The European Imperium voluntarily decided to give the problem of Europe's world-position precedence over that of Europe's internal constitution. It was hoped that solution of the latter problem could be postponed until a time when it could be resolved more easily and without endangering the European world-position. This decision not to occupy the English Island was the personal decision of the Hero who was custodian of the Destiny of Europe during the Second World War. From the time of that decision on, from June, 1941, the European Imperium's invasion of Asiatic Russia was the real war. Europe expended its energy mainly on winning that war, wherein a victory would have secured the Destiny of the European Culture for the coming century.

Now the War could not take its natural course, that corresponding to the organic power-problems, viz., England and Germany versus Russia and Japan, with America and the other colonies either neutral or allied to Europe. Instead, it was forced by the

Washington regime into a distorted form: England and the European colonies attacked Europe from behind while it was struggling for its Cultural-political-economic-social-military-technical survival.

Since the form of the War was unnatural, having stood in no relation to the organic power-problem posed by the power-currents, its results were unnatural, too. As the Organic Laws of Politics show, such a distortion as the Second World War can result only from the intrusion of a Culturally-alien group into the political affairs of the host-organism. The Second World War was the most monstrous manifestation of Culture-distortion in the history of High Culture.

The Culturally-alien group that conjured up the War could symbolize its triumph over the West through the infamous "tribunal" at Nuremberg, a year after the War, but its victory was as unnatural as the War itself. Nor can a Culturally-alien group occupy any kind of lasting political position within the host-organism. It summons forth its own opposition, Cultural antibodies, through which its power will eventually be dissolved. Power, to be perfect, must be openly exercised; however, a Culturally-alien group can hold power only so long as it works through others, through individuals, organizations, classes, governments, and groups of every sort that it manipulates to direct their forces temporarily into its own channels.

Likewise, Russia's ascendancy as a result of the War is unnatural. It does not bring organic actualities to expression, but contradicts them. Europe possesses the true sources of power, which are spiritual-ethical; the Russian Empire is only a formless grouping of barbaric tribes with a purely negative mission. In this, its Imperial Age, Europe is simply not ripe for a long domination by barbarians.

Thus it was a war of spent energies and lost power, of territory lost and cities destroyed, a waste of life, wealth, effort - a waste everywhere but in the realm of Heroism and the Spirit. In the spiritual domain, the great process of forming the Imperium continued unrelentingly, and one saw the curious spectacle of the Washington regime's puppets, the Churchill's, taking up the aim of the Hero they had helped Washington and Moscow to destroy. They began to talk about the "unification of Europe." A few months before they hated the Europe that had been united - indissolubly united through blood spilt on the tundra's and steppes, in the forests of Russia, and to destroy it they were prepared to betray their European Fatherlands and their own souls. After the War, the hottest-headed of the puppets shrieked in horror, in the style of his war-incitements, that Asia now stood at the Elbe. When the frontier was at the Volga and in the Caucasus, he did everything in his power, little as that was, to bring this frontier into the middle of Europe.

76

The Heroic world stands infinitely above the economic-technical disjunction utile-inutile. Nor is the military test of "victory" valid in the realm of Heroism. It was Cromwell who inspired generations of leaders long after his death and subsequent disgrace, not the later Stuarts who had caused his body to be dismembered by wild horses. It was Napoleon who inspired a whole century of leaders after him, not Louis XVIII, nor Metternich, nor Talleyrand. About 1840, Napoleon triumphed, he whose name one could praise in Europe twenty years before only at one's peril. Napoleon's Idea conquered the spiritual-political realm, his personality the Heroic realm. Who would reproach him now with the fact of the lost battles of Leipzig and Waterloo?

So it shall be with the Hero of the Second World War. He represented a new ethical type that will inspire and inwardly form all coming leaders of significance of the West. The bewailing of his "mistakes" after the Second World War was simply contemptible. Every journalist and every braggart knows better than the great man – they would not have made this mistake or that. Indeed, they would never have been in the place to do anything at all!

Heroism is and can never be wasted. So long as men survive a Hero, they will be influenced by him and his legend. He lives on in spirit, and continues to act upon the world of facts and deeds.

THE AMERICAN OCCUPATION OF EUROPE

After the Second World War, the opponents of the Hero of that War were still dominated by his compelling personality. Either they took up his ideas and declared them their own, or they continued to fight against him. Of a new Idea, independent of that Hero, there was not a trace. This can be explained by the issues in world politics being yet the same as those of the Second World War, for the War solved no power-problems, having neither followed nor changed an organic power-current.

During the War, some Europeans entertained the comfortable illusion that the Washington regime was hostile only to certain states in Europe, certain Culture-peoples in Europe, and certain ideas in Europe. Nevertheless, the Washington regime's real enemy was Europe, which means, above all, the Culture-bearing stratum of Europe, that invisible stratum of the population that by virtue of its sensitivity to Cultural Imperatives is the custodian of the Destiny of the Western Civilization, and will remain so, too, until the end of Western history. This stratum of approximately 250,000 souls is distributed throughout Europe, but, naturally, it is concentrated primarily in Germany, which can be attributed to the organic fact that the Prussian-German nation is destined to actualize the European Imperium. Since this stratum is invisible - who could have looked at Rembrandt, Goethe, Napoleon, Bismark in the cradle, and seen what they were to become? -the Washington regime began its post-War task of liquidating this stratum by attempting to kill all of those who had already proved themselves an elite.

Herod sought to kill the Christ Child by slaughtering all male infants in Bethlehem of two years and under. To the invaders it did not seem feasible to take over this technique in its entirety. Yet they believed that if they extinguished the elite of the past they would ipso facto prevent the formation of a new elite, that of the Future. Hence they proceeded with a monstrous Black Mass of scaffold-trials, unique in History, that were intended to kill off everybody whose war-service in a particular field had been of outstanding merit. These Black Masses, variously called "Entnazifizierung," "epuration," and the like, in various countries, were performed in all parts of Europe at behest of the Washington regime. Even in such countries as Sweden and Switzerland, which had not participated in the War, the Washington regime had certain people hunted down, "tried," and killed. By these methods, thousands of the best minds were liquidated. But that was still not enough. Huge masses of human beings had to be butchered. In a certain way, at least, Herod's method had to be applied.

Accordingly, "laws" were devised for ex post facto application: Everyone who in the past believed in the establishment of a European Imperium, and worked for it, was a "criminal." The "penalty" for this "crime" of obeying the Historical Imperative of our Age could not be simple imprisonment for a definite term; that would be impossible. Murder millions by steel and by cord? No, millions of individuals had to be ruined for the rest of their lives.

Hundreds of thousands of French, Walloon, Flemish, Dutch, Danish, and Norwegian soldiers returned home after years of battle against Asiatic Russia and found themselves accused of "treason" and condemned to death or sentenced to years of imprisonment in concentration camps. (In Belgium alone, the Americans incarcerated 400,000 from a population of 8 million.) For under the Neuordnung of the Washington regime, the struggle of Europeans for the survival and power of Europe was designated "treason." Thus an American colonel, acting as a "judge" in a "war-crimes trial," told a European soldier who had carried out the orders of his superior officers: "You could have deserted! "

After being released from the overflowing concentration camps, the "criminals" were robbed of every possession, sentenced to heavy fines, deprived of all civil rights, which made it nearly impossible for them to earn their livelihood, and forbidden to perform any but the meanest sorts of labor.

The American High Command fiercely pursued a policy that brought about a uniform impoverishment of the Europeans to whom it contemptuously referred as "the indigenous population." Years after the War, the High Command deliberately blew up European factories, or dismantled and shipped them to Asiatic Russia; chopped down giant forests in Germany that had provided timber years before Columbus discovered America; confiscated large sections of European cities and forbade Europeans to enter them; drove from their homes, cruelly and unexpectedly, hundreds of thousands of European families so as to make room for those of the occupation soldiers of America and her satellite-regimes; set a daily ration of 1,000 calories for adults, which corresponds to only one third of the amount needed to sustain human life; forbade its occupation soldiers to give or sell Europeans food and clothing, even to speak to them. And, finally, it proclaimed to Europe that the Americans had come as a Herrenvolk, possessed of great understanding for political realities and morality, to liberate "Europeans" and "educate" them up to True Democracy.

Although the American occupation used the slogan "democracy," it did not make even a pretence of introducing 19th century democratic forms. The press, political parties, every kind of gathering, every move - everything required a "License." This was the substitution of a negative, mechanical Fuhrerprinzip for the natural, organic Authoritarian State founded upon the inwardly imperative principles of Ethical Socialism, which is the destined state-form of Europe in this Age of Absolute Politics. This was the tyranny of capitalist liberalism, using the mere methods of the European state-form without understanding their spiritual content. The "freedom of speech" America brought to Europe by conquest is best shown through the example of Bevin, the English Foreign Secretary. In 1948, he spoke publicly of "financial servitude to Wall Street," and within one day, was forced to beg its pardon in public.

The American occupation brought into the open a whole stratum of the European population that had hitherto never been recognized as a unit. In Germany the expression "der Deutsche Michel" has long been current. It pertains to the type with anti-national instincts, an enthusiast for talk instead of action, likewise for anti-social individualism, laissez-faire, and parliamentarism, a person who cringes to aliens, a natural, instinctive, organic, traitor. This stratum of the German population worked systematically but quite instinctively, in two World Wars, for a victory of the enemy. Like the Culture bearing stratum, the Michel-type is distributed Europe-wide. In every

European country, America has an inner-America, the Michel-stratum, as an advertisement for its political success, and pseudo-Europeans it uses to implement its policies locally. Such Europeans are called "Churchill's," after the best known member of their species.

Finally, the American occupation of Europe demonstrated irrefutably that England's policy of "isolation" from the rest of Europe, from the European family of nations to which it belongs, was a grotesque anachronism in the 20th century, the Age of Absolute Politics, of the struggle for control of the planet, wherein only Great Powers with a large geographic basis can take part, not tiny islands situated close to the Continent. In the Age of Economics and Nationalism, the policy of Isolation, likewise the "Balance of Power" idea was justified. Much that was right, correct, natural, and justified in the 19th century is in the 20th century merely past history. In that century, it was possible for England alone to conquer and hold in check India. In this century, that no longer lies within the realm of possibility. In that century, sea-power could be employed decisively. In this century, sea-power is no longer decisive, since the entire hinterland is politically active.

It was tragic that England held so long to the isolation doctrine, for that made possible Washington's policy of a second fratricidal war. The isolation-idea thus contributed its part to the loss of Europe's world hegemony. However, this idea survives today only in the sclerotic brains of Culturally-backward old men. What is decisive is the fact of England's passing, together with all other European countries and peoples, into the common status of subjection to America, not the feigning of unimpaired English sovereignty by a certain stratum left over from the past. England's community of Destiny with the rest of Europe is now patent to everybody in the world, is everywhere binding, and can be denied neither in the individual nor for one moment.

THE DEMISE OF THE WESTERN NATIONS

In one of its results, the Second World War showed the entire world that the Age of Nationalism is forever past. Precisely those nations whose enmities had reached such fantastic proportions in that Age ceased to exist as political units. There is no relation of cause and effect here, for the Nation-Ideas have a certain life-span, just as every aspect of a Culture's existence, and every Western nation died when it was organically its turn. The last phase of a Nation-Idea is its political one.

The oldest of the Western nations, the first to have attained the political phase of its development, was Spain. Its great period began with the unification of Aragon and Castile and reached its summit with the world-ascendancy of Charles V. The last act of Spanish history was the revolt against Napoleon, and even then the resistance was more primitive and racial than national. After that period, Spain no longer played an independent role in Western history, though, of course, it retained a common Destiny with the Western Culture, and was conscious of it. France entered its political phase in the time of Richelieu and appeared in Western history as a spiritually independent people until the turn of the century. The last affirmative act of this nation manifested itself in 1914 at the Marne. Austria was a Great Power from the time of Charles V until 1900, although in the course of the 19th century it became less and less sure of itself. The linguistic form of the Nation-Idea in the Western Culture, which dominated that century, weakened the Austrian Idea to the point where Austria's last independent political act - the ultimatum to Serbia in June, 1914 – was dictated more by pride than politics.

England's political history as a nation extends from Cromwell to Joseph Chamberlain. Before Cromwell, there was no World Idea in England, and after Chamberlain, an Idea no longer existed, could no longer exist, for national extinction, like every other organic phenomenon, is irreversible. Between 1600 and 1900, England's power increased to the extent that in 1900 it controlled by its fleets and armies 17/20ths of the surface of the earth. Spiritually, the entire Western Civilization - particularly from 1750 onwards - was Anglicized. The thought- and action-systems of 19th century were English: Marxism arose on the basis of English capitalist economics; Darwinism reflects the English individualistic-competitive world-outlook; Materialism, Legalism, Capitalism, Social-Ethics - all are of English provenance, and they were the foundations of the 19th century.

The Boer War occurred at the turning-point. At that time, wrote the Englishman Christopher Sykes, England suddenly became the most hated country in Europe. All at once, the spiritual centre-of-gravity shifted: Darwinism succumbed to the Mutation Theory of de Vries, the class-warfare of Marx to the organic State-Socialism of Bismarck, social-ethics to Political Ethics, Sensualist philosophy to the idealist, laissez-faire to state intervention in the economy, Liberalism to the precursors of the Reawakening of Authority, pacifism to the reassertion of martial virtues, and daydreams of an eternal peace were shattered in the global arena of the Age of Absolute Politics.

This was the end of the intellectual-spiritual Anglicization of Europe - but not of America, for colonies have their own organic rhythm, as the History of High Culture shows, and all colonies are perforce Culturally retarded. And it was the beginning of the new Nation-Idea of the West: the entire Culture itself constituted as a Nation, i.e., as an Imperium.

As nations, Germany and Italy were destined by the advent of the new Age, namely that of Absolute Politics, to be stifled before they had yet lived through the mature political phase of their existence. Unlike France, Spain, Austria, and England, however, these two nations are inwardly alive, i.e., their Nation-Idea, their National Mission, is not fulfilled.

Spain fulfilled itself before the Age of Nationalism, France and Austria during that Age, England and the Age of Nationalism unfolded concurrently, and Germany and Italy must fulfill themselves after the Age of Nationalism. Thus these two nations will not fulfill themselves in a nationalistic form in the old sense of the word. They will fulfill themselves as the custodians of the Destiny of all Europe, and the new Nation-Idea of Culture-as-Nation will be the instrument of their fulfillment.

As political units, of course, Germany and Italy are dead. It lies beyond all possibility that one or the other could ever regain its sovereignty except as part of a sovereign Europe. Both stand in the shadow of America and Russia, which falls over all Europe. However, the German and Italian peoples possess the instincts that alone guarantee a role in History. The three great instincts upon which all power is based are: the absolute will to self-preservation, to procreation, and to increasing power. The first and last instincts directly describe super-personal organisms, the second only indirectly through the human beings that compose the body of the higher organism. A nation that welcomes foreign troops is no longer fit to live - such a thing is rendered impossible by the absolute instinct for self-preservation, which excludes submission to any other organism, whether "friend" or "foe." A nation in numerical decline is moribund: the size of the population is the result of the National Mission. A nation that no longer strives for power and possessions is dying, and the actual renunciation of power - even by traitorous Churchill's - means the nation is dead, for a living nation simply does not surrender its power.

The great nation-forming Ethic in this stage of European history is the Prussian-German Idea of Ethical Socialism. Only this living, wordless Idea can banish the overshadowing extra European powers, form the European Imperium, and lead the West to the fulfillment of its World-Mission. Imbued with the new Ethic and free of petty-statist 19th century nationalism, the European nations will climb out of the abyss as a unity, or they will never climb out at all.

Germany is the only surviving nation of Europe that contains formative possibilities, and so it has become identical with the West. Since the Destiny of Europe is at once that of the Imperium, which can take only an Authoritarian Socialist form, Prussia-Germany is the custodian of the Destiny of all Europe. This is an organic fact, and it is wholly independent of human logic or wishes. Destiny is at work in what exists, not what disgruntled old men wish existed.

This relationship of Germany to Europe was confirmed by the Second World War. While the War continued, there was power based in Europe. The very moment the European phase of the War ceased, there was no longer any power in Europe, all power-decisions being made in Washington and Moscow or with their permission. The German resistance to the American Russian invasion was no 19th century nationalism, since the whole Culture-bearing stratum in Europe took part in this struggle and troops for the battles came not only from German-speaking territories, but voluntarily from every other part of Europe as well.

Words that in the 19th century described Nation-Ideas, describe in the 20th century only geographic areas. Today the words German, Spanish, English, Italian, French describe only languages and territories, but no longer peoples, nations, political units or super-personal Ideas. Since a mysterious force inheres in the words when they are used polemically, a policy for European Liberation that would attain success will not use the geographic and linguistic words, England, France, Italy, Spain, Germany in a political sense, but will use the word Europe alone.

The advance of History has destroyed the old significance of these words, and a dynamic policy needs its own terminology. Today 19th century nationalists are the instruments of the occupying forces, which follow the old maxim: Divide et impera. What European would dare speak openly in favor of the American occupation of Europe? What European would declare himself against Europe's organic Unification, against its resurrection as a sovereign unit of Culture-State-Nation-People-Race?

Using the old appellations of nationality, one can say without paradoxical intent that in the 20th century an Englishman, an Italian, a Spaniard is a German. In this century, it is of scant importance what language a European speaks and in what geographic area he was brought up. Of importance only is the spirituality that permeates his inner life. Europe's Churchill's and toy n bees prove that it is possible for Americans to be born and raised in Europe. The example of Mussolini shows that an ethical Prussian can be born and raised in the Romagna, and the examples of Ezra Pound, William Joyce, Robert

Best, Douglas Chandler, and others show that Europeans can be born or raised in America.

In this century the idea of vertical race is dead. We can now view race only in horizontal terms-the race one feels in oneself is everything, the anatomic-geographic group to which one belongs means nothing. In this stage of our Cultural development, the principle of individuality reasserts itself, as it asserted itself in the earliest days of the Gothic. During the dark age of Materialism, it was believed that heredity and environment were everything; with the decline of Materialism the human Soul regains its former dignity. Everyone must now openly admit that the engrafting of the outworn nonsense of the vertical race notion onto the glorious European Resurgence of Authority brought about by the European Revolution of 1933 was an enormous tragedy - all the more so since the coupling of these two ideas was in no way necessary or even logical.

In the Classical Culture, any man who was ethically equal to the Inner Imperative of Roman spirituality could rightly say: "Ciuis Romanus sum". In this, our Western Culture is somewhat akin to the Classical. Our touchstone of comradeship and belonging is spiritual-ethical, not the old one of birth-place, cephalic-index, eye-color. In the 20th century, the century of elective affinities, materialistic tests are pure stupidity.

One last word on the relation of Germany to Europe. The adoption of the German formative-ethic of Authoritarian Socialism by all Europe means, of course, the automatic disappearance of Germany as a petty-state. The Anglicizing of Europe in the 19th century did not mean the Europeanizing of England, for the 19th century was the age of petty-nationalism. However, with the coming to an end of that age, the ethical Germanization of Europe is simultaneously the Europeanization of Germany. In Germany, as elsewhere, petty-stateism is dead. Europe will have a Prussian-ethical Future or none at all. Either Authoritarian Socialism will win its victory and liberate Europe from its enemies, or else Europe will be reduced permanently to Chinese conditions. Either Europe will unite in this Ethical Idea, or it will ever remain a collection of provinces over which the Outer Forces will wage their wars of plunder.

The test of rationality is completely invalid in History; the test in that field is organic possibility As to Politics, Europe has but one organic possibility, the Imperium, and but one Ethic, Authoritarian Socialism. The nations are dead, for Europe is born.

What names this mighty Imperium will bear in History, what language its people will speak, where its capital will be - these are secondary questions for us in the middle of the 20th century, and no one alive today will decide them. All that matters now is that unless Europe forms itself into an indivisible national-political entity by dint of its nation-building Ethic of Authoritarian Socialism, the Europe of 2050 will be essentially the same as that of 1950, viz., a museum to be looted by barbarians; a historical curiosity for sight-seers from the colonies; an odd assortment of operetta-states; a reservoir of human material standing at the disposal of Washington and Moscow; a loan-market for New York financiers; a great beggars' colony, bowing and scraping before the American tourists.

In the face of Europe's terrifying position between the Second and Third World Wars, the old differences between the remnants of the old Nation-Ideas collapse into nothing. Every man of significance in our times is History-oriented, for one cannot profoundly understand our times, their Inner Imperative and Mission, unless one ponders deeply the meaning of Leibnitz' aphorism: Le present est charge du phase et gros de Pavenir. In his inner life, Western man now cannot take sides in the bygone struggles between Wallenstein and Gustavus Adolphus, Olivares and the Cortes, Richelieu and the Fronde, Stuarts and Parliament, Bourbons and Habsburgs, Church and State, England and Spain, Italy and Austria. Today the loftier European identifies himself with both sides in these titanic struggles, with the totality of our precious Western History, for that History is his own spiritual biography written before him in large letters. He, too, had his Gothic, Reformation, Enlightenment, and rationalist-revolutionary phase – his youthful religiosity and crusades, his Democratic-Liberal-Communist phase; and now, in his fullest maturity, he has entered, spiritually and materially, the Age of Absolute Politics, in which the struggle is planetary and its motive Cultural. That means not 19th century petty states and nations, but that only the Culture-State-Nation –Imperium can take part in it.

With its successes and failures, its "flaws" and brilliancy, its advances and retreats, Western History describes ourselves. Even with the First World War, we are still able to experience inwardly what both sides felt. But with the Second World War, the higher type of European experiences only one side, for that War was in its main aspect a war of the West against Asia, and all men of the West who, knowing that, sided against the European Imperium were traitors to the West, inner enemies of their own Culture. In 1914, it was England versus Germany, but in 1939 this was no longer the case. By 1939, the England of Walpole and North, Canning and Gladstone, Kitchener and Joseph Chamberlain was dead and buried. Replacing it was the "England" of Eden and Churchill, Cooper and Belisha - not even a recognizable caricature of the youthful England of the Independents.

These were no far-sighted Empire Builders with unerring power-calculations, but only liquidators of the Empire, American agents, greeters of the "valiant Red Army." As their enemy they named the European Culture, the organism of which England is a vital part and with which it will always share a common Destiny. Every English statesman of the old tradition would have recognized the growth of events during the third decade of the 20th century from a European to a global scale. But these wretched epigoni with their boundless jealousy and muddled instincts closed their eyes to it and sold the English Island to the Washington regime for a little pseudo-power and the fleeting glory of a suicidal "victory."

In this historical orientation, the Westerner of the higher type, who alone has Cultural value and significance, regards events in which the West was pitted against the Outer Forces with a completely subjective eye. Thus he sees in the Crusades, for example, only one side of the question - I am speaking here not of any ethical, religious, moral, aesthetic, or other such questions, of course, but solely of the organic question of identity. He is for Charles XII against the Russians, for England against the Indian Mutiny, against the Zulus, and against China in the Opium War; for the Teutonic Knights against the Slav at Tannenberg; for Maximilian against Juarez; for the American Colonists in the Alamo against Santa Ana; for Napoleon against Russia; for Mussolini against the negroes of Abyssinia; for the Hero and his Army against Russia in 1941-1945. In these events, it was left only to chance which of the Western nationalities fought the Barbarian. The victory of any Western nation over an outer military force, whether Chinese, Hindu, Zulu, Islamic, was a victory for all Europe and its colonies. Any European who gloats over the defeat of a Western nation brands himself politically and Culturally feeble-minded. For what distinction does the Barbarian make between the Western nations? During the Second World War, the Japanese called the Germans "friendly enemies" and the English "hostile enemies." To Jewry all men of the West are "goyim;" to Islam they are "giaours" and "Franks," and in Persia during the First World War Walmus had the greatest difficulty in making clear to the tribal chieftains why the two "Frankish" powers were fighting each other. For a European to emphasize any trifling differences between the Western nations today is stupidity, if not treason.

Yet Anglophobia, the mode of yesterday, is back in style again; Germanophobia has been transformed by the Outer Forces of Washington and Moscow into a veritable hate-religion for the masses. In this direction lies the Sinoization of Europe.

Treasonous propaganda in Europe between the Second and

Third World Wars has its origin with the Outer Enemies of Europe. Spreading it is taken care of by the Inner Enemy of Europe.

THE INNER ENEMY OF EUROPE

An inner enemy is more dangerous than an outer one, because while he seems to belong, he is actually a kind of alien.

The Inner Enemy of Europe is at once a stratum of the population, a world-outlook, and a Culture-illness. The Michel-stratum is Europe's Inner Enemy, the stratum that commits treason organically and instinctively. Its world-outlook is that of the past Age of Nationalism, Economics, Democracy, Capitalism. Because it looks backward and resists the Imperative of the Future with pathological intensity, this stratum is the embodiment of the Culture-disease called Culture-retardation.

An inner enemy is dangerous in two respects: first, because of his own activity, and, second, because of his usefulness to the outer enemy. During the Second World War, the European Michel consciously worked for the defeat of Europe and the victory of the American-Russian coalition. Examples of this conduct were Churchill and Attlee in England, Badoglio and Mauggeri in Italy, Halder, Hassel, and Goerdeler in Germany, the Communists in France, the Netherlands, Spain, and Scandinavia. Without this organic, professional treason on the part of the European Michel, the Outer Forces could never have defeated Europe. After the War, the American occupation of Europe and the despoliation of Europe were made possible only by the Michel-stratum, which hired itself out to the enemy to establish vassal-governments, Churchill-regimes, in every province of Europe. During this period between the Second and Third World Wars, the Michel as an American agent is more dangerous than he would otherwise be in himself. The reason for this is the advance of History since the 19th century has rendered his world-outlook completely useless to him, even for purposes of sabotage, while to the Americans it is still useful as a means of control over Europe. Thus the Culture-disease of Culture-retardation remains in the body of Europe only because of the American occupation.

If "capitalism" is understood not simply as an economic technique, but, above all, as a spiritual-ethical principle, we may designate the world-outlook of the Michel as Capitalism. In the 20th century, Capitalism is inwardly dead, both in the broader sense of a Cultural-ethical world-outlook and as an economic technique. The fact that it is dead is shown every time its representatives approach some new problem in the world of facts. Their solutions are uniformly rigid and in every case misfire, even when the problem is purely economic.

After the Second World War, the English government that called itself "socialist" decided to "nationalize" the railways. The sole possible raison d'être for nationalization of the railways lay in reducing costs for the ultimate consumer, thus granting a sort of general rebate. But there resulted a doubling of all fares and a continuation of the separate identity of the lines, even to the point of competitive advertising. The program remained in existence only for the sake of the principle of nationalization. All other "nationalization" schemes that originated with this capitalistic, class-war inciting Marxist regime ended similarly.

The singularly unhappy career of the capitalist system was continued throughout Europe after the Second World War, to be sure, because of intervention coming from the Culture-periphery. Unhesitatingly, the Washington regime employed the resources of the North American continent to shore up the tottering system. Thus it is only the extra-European power of the Washington regime that subjects Europe to the negative world-outlook and outworn economic system of capitalism. A European revolt against capitalism is ipso facto a revolt against America. A Socialist Europe, founded on the principle of the sovereign, organically articulated State, would be an independent Europe and master of its own economy. This economy would not be established for reasons of class-war, nor for the purpose of realizing any rigid, abstract ideas. On the contrary, it would be an economy that overcomes the economic problems of Europe in the spirit of the 20th century, and, indeed, in their sole possible way of solution: the State as organism and its economy as part of an organic totality to which all private and class interests are subordinate.

Before the First World War, the European power-monopoly, the monopoly of trade and technics, secured all requisite markets for the products of Europe, and with these products Europe paid for the raw and other materials it ordered from abroad. The First World War undermined this system in that, for its duration, it deprived the overseas consumers of European merchandise, and thus gave them the stimulus to construct factories of their own. After the War, the capitalist international economy was never again able to solve its problems, not even through extensive state-intervention in the form of protective tariffs, and the like. This development was concluded by the Second World War. The old system passed away.

The only solution for the economic problems of Europe consists in the most intensive possible rationalization of all existing possessions and in the acquisition of new resources for the European economy. Naturally, America insists that Europe keep the capitalist system. A Socialist Europe does not need America, whereas a capitalist Europe is a beggars' colony of America.

In the basic world-outlook of both the American population and the ruling economic caste the world is still the object of plunder. America is not interested in forming and organizing the world, but in creating the widest possible opportunities for financial-economic penetration of other countries. It is driven even to military conquest to attain this goal securely. Again, this is 19th century motivation, and its corrosive, pathological revival in our Age is a symptom of Culture-retardation.

To the finance-capitalist politico-military thought is merely a tool, albeit that it may seem to predominate at times. It is a dangerous weapon. The possibility is ever present that a political general might like to rule the roost. The political general is the nightmare of the finance-capitalist, and therein lies the explanation for the inferior businessman-type and feebleminded liberals that make up the American generalcy. All officers of strong will and superior intellect are weeded out before they attain to the rank of general; and in 1941 the Army regulations were so revised that automatic promotion to general - which had been the rule in the American Army since its beginnings in the 18th century – was eliminated, and promotion to that rank made dependent on "service," i.e., subservience to the Washington regime, or in other words, on the lack of any earnest will and strong instincts.

To recapitulate everything: the Inner Enemy of Europe may be described in three ways:

1. With regard to his Culture-biological value.
2. With regard to which stratum embodies him.
3. With regard to his conception of the world.

> 1. The Inner Enemy is the bearer of Culture-retardation.
> 2. The Inner Enemy is the Michel-stratum; his leaders are the Churchill's.
> 3. The Inner Enemy is Capitalism, whereby the word is used in its total meaning of a Cultural-spiritual-ethical-economic principle.

In contrast to the foregoing, the true European spirit may be likewise sketched:

1. It is Culture-health, i.e., the actualization of the Inner Imperative, accepting the challenge of the Future.
2. It is in the charge of the Culture-bearing stratum, the highest elite of

the population, which stratum comprises no more than circa 250,000 souls.

3. It is the grand Idea of Imperialism, the world-outlook that is suited to the coming European Imperium of Culture-State-Nation-People-Race-Society.

For the purpose of demonstrating with the utmost clarity the elements of the two world-outlooks in this period of Western History between the Second and Third World Wars, a paradigm is appended:

Imperialism	*Capitalism*
Faith	Rationalism
Primacy of the Spirit	Materialism
Idealism	Sensualism
Will-to-Power	Will-to-Riches
World as object of organization	World as object of plunder
Rank as social distinction	Wealth as social distinction
Society as organism	Society as a collection of individuals
Fulfillment of Duty	"Pursuit of happiness"

Ascendant instincts:	*Decadent instincts:*
1. Absolute Western self-preservation	1. Acquiescence to the Outer Revolt
2. Absolute will to biological fertility	2. Race-suicide, birth control, Puritanism, Bohemianism
3. Absolute will to increase Power	3. Surrender of the World hegemony of the West

Hierarchy	*Equality*
Discipline	Freedom, ethical laissez-faire
Authority	Parliamentarianism
The super-personal organism as state	The super-personal organism as society
Aristocracy	Plutocracy
Society as an organic unity	Class-war
Sexual polarity	Feminism
Europe as Imperium	Petty-statism
Europe as Nation	Chauvinism
Europe as Fatherland	Petty-nationalism

Order	Freedom
Stability	Constant motion, business cycles
Responsibility, all public Power exercised and administered openly	Irresponsibility, anonymity, public power in the hands of private persons, finance Capitalists, labor-dictators
Resurgence of Authority	Communism, Democracy Liberalism
Ideal of Chivalry, faith in Oneself	Separation of Word and deed, systematic hypocrisy
Respect for the political Enemy	Replacement of respect by hatred, "war crimes trials", Ideals as a substitute for Honor on the battlefield
Cultivation of soldierly Virtues	Cult of bourgeois virtues, the derision of soldierly virtues
Eroticism as legitimate source of joy and fertility	Eroticism as vice, the cult of immorality, general spread of clandestine and illegal prostitution, an erotic without consequences
Affirmation of War and Conquest	Pacifism, preparation of the colored populations for "self-government" the "right to self-determination"
Separate status of culture-alien	Equality with the Culture alien, the "melting pot"
Western Man as an individual Human being, completely Different from primitive Non-western humans, Western man in the service Of a great mission: the Fulfillment of the European	Rousseau: Man as Savage Darwin: Man as animal Marx: man as economic creature Freud: Man as sexual creature Science-as-religion: man as machine,

Culture	capable of limitless Existence, "victory over Disease," etc.
Art practiced in conformity with the Cultural task	"L'art pour l'art"
Politico-military expansion	Financial-military-economic expansion

From a cursory glance at the list of examples it is obvious that the reigning forces of Culture-retardation make use of the ideas and instincts of Imperialism whenever and wherever they find it necessary and possible. For instance, they subordinate Art to Politics. They have set up a new, inverted hierarchy in which the American and the Michel are the patricians and the true European is the plebeian. They preach "democracy" while ruthlessly imposing their will on the masses and pressuring them in so called elections; they deny the rightness of the Idea of Conquest while occupying Europe with their troops and forcing its people to take on heavy political, military, and economic burdens in the interest of the extra-European powers, and so on.

This is the Age of Absolute Politics, and everyone who acts in this Age, acts in its spirit, whether he knows it or not, whether he wishes it or not. If he reflects, makes use of, values that run counter to his stated political beliefs and aims, then he is either hopelessly stupid or is pursuing some other goal than the fulfillment of the Destiny of Europe - the formation of the Western Imperium in the spirit of Ethical Socialism.

There are two designs here: the first is the design of the European Michel, who seeks only his own advantage (the Churchill's) or that of his class (the finance-capitalist class; the proletarian usufructuaries of the looting of the body of Europe). The second design is that of the Cultural-outsider, the total alien, who in his boundless rancor directs a political will-to-annihilation against the West, who negates its Inner Imperative, who would strangle its Destiny and divert it from the Future. Geographically, he may act from outside the Western Culture, or inside, in the form of Culture-distortion. In each case, it is his spirituality that clinches the matter, and the Culture-distorter is one of the Outer Enemies of Europe.

THE OUTER ENEMIES OF EUROPE

When used in Politics, the word enemy has a meaning completely different from what it has when used in regard to Culture or private life. In private life, we call him our enemy who bears us ill will. Applied to world politics, this definition is meaningless, for no state bears ill will in any private sense. That is true even in those cases in which a political unit is animated by a purely negative will, and would express it politically. For the form-world of Politics itself conditions all political activity and transforms its whole content into power activity. However, Politics seldom does supply its own motivation - that is to be sought in another realm.

The motivation of the global power-struggle in our Age of Absolute Politics lies in Culture. On the planet there is only one High Culture in the process of fulfillment, the Western Culture, and as a spiritual front it naturally assumes the following form: the West against the Outer Revolt. The spiritual motivation of the politics of all outer forces whatever is the will-to-annihilate the Western Culture. In a power struggle between Europe and any outer force, each contestant will, however, strive for power, that means control over the other. The motivation of the contestants will become apparent only after a power decision in the struggle. Thus it is obvious that the West does not have the desire to destroy the peoples, territories, resources, and low cultures of the outer forces, whereas these outer forces most emphatically wish to destroy the peoples, landscape, resources, and the High Culture of Europe, as the Russian-American occupation of Europe after the Second World War demonstrated.

In the purely spiritual sense, then, Europe has but one "enemy," the Outer Revolt against the World Hegemony of the West. From this great, fundamental fact we know that the Outer Revolt will provide Europe with political enemies so long as the Age of Absolute Politics lasts. A European victory in the struggle for the planet will not extinguish the Outer Revolt as a spiritual front; it will simply prevent it from again rising to the level of political intensity. At present, this spiritual front is divided into two political units: Russia and America-Jewry. Culturally, it is anomalous that America and one of the outer enemies of Europe are interdependent, for America belongs by its origin and fate to the Western Culture. All the same, it must now be counted among the enemies of Europe, since ethically and politically it is dominated by the Culture-alien Jewish entity of Church-State-Nation-Society-Race. Just how this domination came about is of less concern to Europe than the fact of it. The objective events of world history since 1933 show that in not one instance has America pursued an American nationalist policy, but exclusively a policy in the interests of the Jewish entity.

In order to bring the metapolitical realities of this period between the Second and Third World Wars into clearer focus, each of the Outer Enemies of Europe must be examined separately.

America is, and shall always be, a colony of the Western Culture. A colonial spirituality determines the fate of colonies. So it has been with every previous Culture. When on the Home-soil the parent-Culture becomes extinct, everywhere the colonies perish. Population-streams may continue in primitive form; landscapes, of course, remain, but they are desolate and tyrannize the human beings that just yesterday dominated them; edifices may yet stand, but their symbolism is no longer understood. A colony is linked by a mystical bond, as though by a spiritual umbilical cord, to the parent organism, a bond just as inexplicable and just as real as the one that binds the Culture to the soil on which it was born. A colony thus shares a common history with the parent-organism, and its life reflects - with a natural and organic retardation - the development of the Culture. In the case of America, this retardation generally corresponds to the life duration of one generation. This lagging behind is not the same thing as Culture-retardation, for it is natural and unavoidable. Still, that tardiness is serviceable to the Culturally-parasitic group which is now contriving to prevent the American colony from reflecting the development of its parent organism. This pathological design is unattainable, of course, but any such deviation from Culture-health must have enormous effects on the host before the parasite is expelled.

The Jewish entity is a Cultural form-world of its own stamp, and can therefore **never** be assimilated by the Western Culture. Since this entity finds itself inside the West - geographically speaking - and since it must seek its political actualization, it necessarily influences Western politics in the direction of its own interests. Though it be of alien origin, it must not appear alien; its politics must be regarded as though it were legitimate politics, and not the alien politics it is. The Western ideology of the 18th and 19th centuries was admirably suited to the political needs of the Jewish entity, but with the passing away of that ideology and the birth of the Age of Absolute Politics, the preconditions for the successful political activity of the Jewish entity on European soil completely vanished. The fictive constructs of "Liberte, Egalite, Fraternite" have entirely died out in Europe; hence the political history of the Jews, as quasi-members of the Western nations, has also ended. Even so, the colonial tardiness in Cultural development and the disease of Culture-retardation make it possible for Jewry to retain its uncontested domination over the American people.

In this period of history, America and Jewry form a Symbiosis. The head of the organism is the Jewish entity, the body is America.

The problem of the existence-duration of this Symbiosis is of only secondary importance to Europe. No one predicted the French Revolution in regard to its time or its form. No one predicted the Russian Revolution of 1917, or the European Revolution of 1933, or the American Revolutions of 1775 and 1933. No one can in any way presage the time or the form of a Third Revolution in America which will take the power away from the Jewish entity and place it in the hands of a new American ruling-stratum. That Revolution is an organic possibility - indeed, even more: it is an organic Unavoidable. But since the time of its outbreak is still an Imponderable, the possibility of such a Revolution can play no role in the formation of Europe's policy, for a policy cannot be based upon Imponderables, though it must be flexible enough to adapt itself when they emerge from the realm of the Unforeseen. When the Revolution starts, it will bring in America a re-awareness of European politics and a re-evaluation of Europe's meaning.

The Symbiosis of America and Jewry in this moment of history between the Second and Third World Wars is decisive not only for America, but also for Jewry. During the centuries of its "dispersion," the Jewish entity never attained to the position of absolute sovereign over the fate of a Western host-people. But now it has come to that, and Jewry has identified itself for political purposes with America before all the world. In that Jewry became the overlord of America, it lost the most important of its other possessions and bases. Before the Jewish hegemony over America, the height of Jewish power was in Bolshevist Russia. In 1945, the superficial observer might have gained the impression that the total political power of the planet was being gradually collected into one political unit. That was in fact the aim of the Jewish leadership, and the means of creating the "world government" was to be the resurrected "League of Nations."

As has already been shown in IMPERIUM, a world-state is an organic impossibility, and likewise a logical one. State is a political term, and political power results from polarity. A state is thus a unit of opposition. Although in theory a world-state would not have an opposition, if one were founded, it would at that very instant split into two or more political units. These would develop along regional, cultural, class, or economic lines - even along the lines dictated by a dominant political figure. Ignoring the concrete example of failure afforded by the "League of Nations" after the First World War, the Jewish-American Symbiosis attempted through its "United Nations" to create a power-monopoly for itself.

One great obstacle was present: Russia. It had been hoped, even taken for granted, that Russia would remain sufficiently under the control of the Jewish entity to collaborate in the scheme and, together with America, formally surrender its legal sovereignty to the "United Nations." But the rise of the American-Jewish Symbiosis undermined the position of the fragment of the Jewish "diaspora" in Russia. So long as Jewry acted alone, it was politically effective in Russia. The worldwide identification of Jewry with America aroused Russian nationalism, with the result that the Culture-alien Jewish entity of Church-State-Nation-Society-Race lost its status as a member, so to speak, of the Russian national structure and was re-classified as a foreign element, thus losing completely its political effectiveness inside Russia.

As we have seen, the sole great spiritual-Cultural "enemy" Europe has is the Outer Revolt, against the West, the great No to the Western World-Mission, and this spiritual-Cultural front is divided into two political units, of which Russia is the second. Between the First and the Second World Wars, Russia was generally acknowledged to be the leader of the Outer Revolt, but in the Russo-Japanese War, 1904-1906, it was vice versa. At that time, Russia figured as a Western power against the Outer Revolt, which was led by Japan as the only sovereign power outside the Western Culture. In between lies the Bolshevist Revolution of 1917.

The Bolshevist Revolution was more than political; it was Cultural. Power was transferred from the Westernized elements in the church, state, army, aristocracy, and intelligentsia to a group basing itself upon the instinctively nihilistic stratum of the Russian peasant masses. The primitive Russian Soul, unsure of itself, had been forced by the Romanovs and the powerful inroads of German culture in Russia to submit to Westernization. Consequently, there arose in Russia a dreadful tension of polarity between the two Souls, the Western and the proto-Russian. Dostoievsky's The Possessed depicts how it fermented nihilistically beneath the surface. It was this underground Russia that, led by the Jewish entity, broke away in 1917 from the West. By 1923, the civil wars had ended, and Western culture was for the time banished from Russia. A community of destiny with Asia and its revolt against the West, rather than with a Europe whose form-world it had just expelled from Russian soil, more nearly answered the expectations of the new Russia.

The Russian Soul is too virile ever to be strangled by something alien. Hence the Jewish entity, despite the dominant position to which it had attained with the Revolution of 1917, was incapable of maintaining its unconditional rule. The expulsion of Trotsky in 1928 marks the downward turning point for Jewry in Russia.

And yet the Bolshevist Revolution did not eliminate the polar tension within the Russian Soul. So long as the Russian Soul, chaotic and full of longing, animated by a strong will yet of weak resolve, exists within the sphere of influence of a Western organism that is conscious of its World-Mission, there will remain in Russia a powerful urge towards reunion with the West. The European Revolution of 1933 found an echo in Russia, and when the European armies entered Bolshevist territory in 1941, they were hailed everyplace there as "liberators." Marshal Vlasov could have raised armies of millions and affiliated them with the European military forces, but, unfortunately, the European Command did not make use of such aid until it was too late. The possibility indeed exists that a second monstrous upheaval - with a pro-Western Cultural aim - will overthrow the Bolshevist regime. This possibility might be realized either through a renewed Western invasion or through the appearance of a new Peter the Great. It is a further Imponderable. Today Europe must reckon with Russia as part of the Outer Revolt against its World-Mission.

Since there are only two political powers in the world, the world situation can assume only the form of preparation for war between them: America-Jewry versus Russia.

If Bolshevism is understood as the urge to destroy the Western Culture, then these two extra-European powers form an anti-Cultural Interregnum in Western History, the Concert of Bolshevism. Both powers are formless and personal; neither is the expression of a super-personal Soul, a higher Destiny, an organically necessary Imperative to a World-Mission. The Outer Forces, whatever the extent to which they have Western technics at their disposal, whatever Western customs they practice, whatever superficial display of literary connections with the West they make, are, in fact, to be classed in the same category with the formless powers of Tamerlane and Genghis Khan, Sun Yat-sen and Kemal Ataturk, Lobengula and the Mahdi. Europe is still the bearer of a World-Idea, a great World-Hypothesis; it still has an inward necessity to view the world in a particular fashion, an Ethic whereby it conducts itself towards it in a particular fashion and reconstructs it in a particular fashion. For the single, all encompassing reason of this total difference between Europe, on the one hand, and the formless extra-European powers on the other, Europe can have at bottom no interest in the projected Third World War within the Concert of Bolshevism per se. Nor would it make any difference in this if the War broke out in 1960 or 1975.

Nevertheless, Europe is linked politically to the projected Third World War, and it must exploit every possibility in the diplomatic preparations for that war to push through its Liberation. Europe must recall its Destiny and its World Mission. It must assess the differences between the two powers in the Concert of Bolshevism, and adapt itself so that it will profit from their changing fortunes in the events to come. Europe must form its policy.

THE DEFINITION OF ENEMY

As we have seen, the word "enemy" has a different meaning when applied to Culture, private life, Politics. In the Cultural sense, Europe has only one "enemy," and that is the Outer Revolt against the World-Mission of the West. It embraces all primitive populations, even in those cases in which they live geographically within the Western Culture, as in North and South America, and includes all fellah-populations now inhabiting areas where High Cultures once fulfilled themselves, for example, the Islamic, Hindu, and Chinese populations. Likewise it embraces populations in whose areas a High Culture has never existed, for example, the barbaric Russians and Mongols, the savages of Africa, South East Asia, and the Pacific islands. The Jewish entity comes from the Magian Culture and will always belong to it spiritually, that Magian Culture which during its life-span gave rise to the Arabian, Persian, Nestorian, and Parsic peoples, among others. While some of these entities may have lost individuals to the West, alien units cannot be assimilated by the West in their entirety. Super-personal realities on both sides forbid it. It is an organic impossibility. The worldwide Cultural front against the West is divided into two political units, Russia and America-Jewry, and the word enemy is used quite differently in Politics.

Politics means so living life that its possibilities are exhausted. In the course of events, Politics divides its world into political friends and political enemies. Before Politics undertakes this division, all outer units are potential enemies, and it is the task of Politics to select one or more units as enemies, then, if possible, to win the other units as friends.

The choice of enemy is the most important decision in the entire realm of activity called Politics. The mighty English Empire, which dominated the world for more than a century, foundered on its simple but profound mistake of choosing the wrong enemy in two World Wars. The whole adroit ancillary diplomacy, the total war-effort, and the military victory itself did not succeed in preventing the disappearance of the greatest Empire in history and the destruction of England's own sovereignty. The English homeland was not even spared the ultimate humiliation of occupation by foreign troops, and, what is more, these troops came from its erstwhile colony. The formulation of policy is esoteric, and this is proved by the selfsame example: Notwithstanding the collapse and disappearance of the

English Empire, notwithstanding the reduction of England itself to the status of an "unsinkable aircraft carrier" for foreign air-forces, the Culture retarding stratum and the broad masses were successfully persuaded by foreign propaganda that a great "victory" had somehow been won for England.

Political blunders can be made at two levels: at the highest level, where the enemy is determined and friends can be obtained, or at the lowest, where the policy based thereupon is carried out. The word error, in the strict sense, can be used in Politics only with regard to the future. Thus one must reproach England for choosing Germany as its enemy in the Second World War when it was obvious that its choice was an error. The great von Moltke defined strategy as "the art of making one less error than your adversary." This definition can be likewise applied to Politics. Considered in retrospect, Life is a fabric of errors. No one can foresee the Future.

Politics is concrete; it is the art of the possible, not of the desirable, not of the moral, not of what is worthy of aspiration. Politics is an art, and it is the grandest of all arts, since its material is human life and its completed work the blossoming of a super-personal Destiny. When a work of art is executed by an inferior, an imitator, an academic, the result is a piece of bungling. The indispensable gift of the politician is the gift of vision; after it, comes finesse in political activity. Without prior vision, the whole fateful proceeding comes to naught.

A statesman comes nearest to the gift of vision when he is aware of his own strength of will and that of his people and perceives the power currents of the political world. A steady adherence to both of these fundamentals will preserve him from the far-reaching error of choosing the wrong enemy. It is tantamount to waging war against oneself. In the Second World War, England sacrificed both the remnants of its Empire and its own independence for the benefit of America and Russia. There are still people who would deny this fact, but only facts are positive, not the sclerotic opinions of half-blind dotards.

The Political Genius is a superlative artist, and thus free of all negativity in his creations. To his task he brings no hatred, no malice, no envy, nor any will-to-destruction that does not serve his will-to-power and will-to-creation. He is incapable of pursuing a policy that is basically "anti"- oriented, for example, a policy that has the slogan "Win the War!" as its "war-aim." Such slogans may have certain propaganda value for the policy of a political Genius, but only the shamelessly hate-filled reactionary of the Churchill sort makes a policy of his hatred and asserts that "victory" at the cost of self-destruction is something worth seeking. Naturally, the political Genius removes from his path all forces opposing him, so far as he can; but this "anti"-tactic he employs for the sake of increasing his power, not from jealousy, prejudice, hatred, or mere dislike.

The problem of choosing an enemy is the same for Europe today, i.e., for the Culture-bearing stratum, as it would be for us if Europe were constituted as an actual political unit. Today Europe is an area and a People, if it pursues the right policy, tomorrow it will be a power - by virtue of its Inner Imperative alone, which proceeds from the unfulfilled Destiny of the Western Civilization. The fact that Europe has a World-Mission guarantees that it will play a role in the centuries to come. Whether this role will be an active one, or merely passive, will become evident in our decades, and will be determined by the policy of the European Culture-bearing stratum.

The choice of an enemy is not arbitrary: We can designate a political unit as enemy only if, first, we can overcome that unit, and, second, by overcoming it gain power. Clearly, in this second Interbellum-Period Europe cannot overcome any power militarily because there does not and cannot exist a European military force as long as Europe is not constituted as a sovereign state. Any military force directly or indirectly under the command of the Washington regime cannot be called a "European military force." The nationality of an army is that of its political leadership, not of its common soldiers or its officer-corps. In these circumstances, Europe is compelled to win power by spiritual-intellectual means. It must extract power from one or both of the Outer Forces, Russia and America-Jewry. That one of these two units from which Europe can draw true political power, viz., unlimited control over its own land and people, is the political enemy. It cannot be emphasized enough that the enemy-definition does not entail, from the European standpoint, any judgment of especially bad ethical, moral, aesthetic, or cultural qualities on the part of the enemy. Culturally, aesthetically, morally, ethically, there is no choosing between Russia and America-Jewry. Yet, politically, Europe is compelled to distinguish between them, by its organic necessity to translate its Inner Imperative into action. It would be impossible for Europe to play a passive role in History, even if it wished, or it were wiser to do so. While Life advances, there is no standing still.

The Definition of Enemy is a problem that must be solved in the total historical frame-of-reference of our Epoch. Thereby the power-currents of the century, the power-problems resulting there from, and the relative danger for Europe must be considered.

THE POWER-PROBLEMS OF
THE SECOND INTERBELLUM PERIOD

Owing to the false form of the first two World Wars and to the presence of a Culture-disease in the Western Civilization, the power-problems in this period between the Second and the Third World Wars are the same ones that have confronted Europe for half a century, but now intensified to the highest possible degree.

In the year 1914, the power-problems were the following: how to preserve Europe's world-hegemony and how to make possible the conversion of Europe from an accumulation of petty-states with the hand-me-down world-outlook of a nationalist-capitalistic parliamentarism to the determined shape of Europe for the 20th century, viz., an Authoritarian Socialist structure of Culture-Nation-People-Race, the Imperium of the West. The form of the First World War, shaped by Culture-retarders like Grey, prevented a natural, organic solution of this power problem.

Between the First and Second World Wars, important steps were taken within Europe for the organic solution of the second problem, the transition of the 20th century phase of the European organism into the world of reality. Hardly anything was done for the solution of the first problem, owing to the precarious world situation at that time, although the Italian Abyssinian War did bring a general increase in power for Europe.

But this organic move forward was halted by the meddling of America-Jewry in intra-European affairs, and, as we have seen, this meddling brought about, in the same sterile form as the First World War, the tragedy of the Second World War. About 1939, the power-problems consisted in the re-establishment of the world-hegemony that had been almost entirely destroyed by the First World War, and in the completion of the half actualized Imperium of Europe. The Second World War, occasioned by the extra-European, non-Western force of America-Jewry and by the Churchill's of France and England, once again thwarted the organic solution of these two problems.

As a result of the Second World War, it can be seen that the power-problems are essentially the same two. Only their order of precedence has changed, so that now the problems are, first, the Liberation of Europe from extra-European rule, for the entirety of Europe is ruled from alien capitals; and, second, the fulfillment of Europe's World-Mission, i.e., the reconquest of its world-hegemony and the establishment of its World Empire.

Every power-problem contains a disjunction between the distribution of spiritual power-sources, on the one hand, and the distribution of acknowledged power and its attributes on the other. The spiritual power-source - the possession of a World-Mission, a calling, a mighty, positive Inner Imperative, and a nation-forming ethic - are found concentrated almost entirely in Europe. The spiritual resources that exist outside Europe, in Russia, America-Jewry, and Japan, are merely a reflex of the European - a European Will that is inspired there by Europe. In actuality, the Outer Forces are seeking to realize the World-Mission of Europe, even though they lack the Inner Imperative to it. Their motivation is completely negative. Thereby is explained the circumstance that the immense concentration of power in the Washington and Moscow regimes has brought no Order to the world, that both regimes perpetuate the Chaos left over in the 20th century from the 19th century. Only Europe can give back to this chaotic world the Principle of Order.

THE AMERICAN POWER ACCUMULATION

The American power-accumulation can be called an "empire" only in a loose, transferred sense. Within the Symbiosis America-Jewry, neither the Jewish entity nor the subordinate American element thinks in terms of American Imperialism. Thus the American head-of-state specifically declared to the populace that no people on earth was in any sense subject to America, that America's "defense" of other peoples did not entitle it to demand reciprocity from them, and, moreover, that under no circumstances would America "dominate" another people. What is of particular significance in this is the anti-imperialist ideology, not the fact that all these principles are completely disregarded in the political conduct of America-Jewry. The intention here is to prevent the rise of American Imperialist thinking, for that would run counter to the anti-nationalist policy of the dominant part of the Symbiosis. But if the Imperialist urge within the American people were of deep, imperative force, and pregnant with the Future, it could not be suppressed, and the power-accumulation that the Washington regime at present administers would be organized into an American Empire.

However, a true American Empire that is hierarchically organized and politically administered will never be, since it is not among the formative possibilities of the American character. Now, a nation cannot arise by happenstance - a people, yes - but a nation is the out flowing of a High Culture. Though America can never belong to any other Culture than the Western, in American life Western culture is only a veneer. Its inward influence on the American population was too slight, for example, to have prevented the invasion of Culturally-alien units. There is no American Idea, no American nation, no American ruling stratum - three ways of expressing the same thing. To be sure, there is an American People, whose members are in fact characterized by an individual imperialism, which is instinctive, racial and economic. But this individual imperialism can never lift itself to political heights. The true American People is a unit based upon matriarchy. By its own choice, it leads a cocoon-like life within a closed system. The soul of this People is too oriented to the feminine pole of existence, and it therefore cherishes peace, comfort, security, in short, the values of individual life. War, conquest, adventure, the creation of form and order in the world - these do not interest the American People. Empire-building demands sacrifices; yet, for sacrifices to be made, and not just sacrificial victims slaughtered, there must be an Idea.

The American power-accumulation arose without sacrifices through America's chance intervention at two decisive moments in world affairs. In the First World War, America's sole war-aim - according to the public and private utterances of all leading Americans who were in favor of intervention in that War - was to defeat "German tyranny." As was shown in the analysis of Politics in IMPERIUM, to have the defeat of an arbitrarily chosen enemy as a "war-aim" is to have no war-aim at all. Thus America had no political aim in that War. The role England played in America's entry into the War is not important here. Important only is the stock of ideas that were played out to set the American People in motion. In the Second World War, America's internal propaganda was exclusively non-political. Again, the chief "war-aim" was to "defeat Germany," and the one attempt to display a positive "war-aim" was a series of negative proposals - all of them reflecting the feminine values of a matriarchy - to free the world of hunger, fear, etc. The psychological orientation of the American People prevents American governments in peacetime from clearly expressing a demand for war. In wartime, it is obligatory to speak only of "peace." "Victory" is supposed to bring only "peace," and not an extension of power. Above all, the purpose of victory is not an American Empire. After the extinction of the Federalist Party in 1828, no political grouping in America publicly advocated the creation of an American Empire. The average type of party-politician ensures, however, that every public man would advocate political imperialism were the idea popular.

The American power-accumulation in this epoch between the Second and Third World Wars has arisen without sacrifice. Had sacrifice been necessary for it, then it would not have arisen.

Before 1914, America controlled only a small section of the world surface: the North American Continent, Central America below Mexico, small areas of northern South America. Not even the

Caribbean Sea could be called American, since European bases were numerous there and the American fleet was inferior in number to more than one European fleet. In the First World War, 10,000,000 men lost their lives on the battlefield. Of this total sum America's tribute amounted to 120,000; for this slight toll in blood, America acquired sufficient new territories and bases, obtained enough power for itself at sea, to have 1/5th of the earth's surface under its control: North America, the whole of Central America, including Mexico, the entire Caribbean, much of South America, and half the Pacific. After the War, in accordance with the feminine-matriarchal orientation of the American People, the greater part of these power-acquisitions was abandoned - this occurred through the Washington Naval Treaty of 1921, under which America obligated itself to sink half its fleet without demanding the equivalent from England or Japan. Yet the fact remains: America acquired a power-area that was four times larger than its original with the vanishingly small blood-toll of 120,000.

By 1939, America had gained control, pari passu with the steady decline of England's power, of 1/5 of the earth-surface. At the end of the Second World War, America controlled 18/20ths of it. That is the largest power-accumulation ever to come about in the entire history of High-Cultures. The total number of dead of all belligerent states amounted to approximately 15 million. America's portion of this loss was 250,000. In the Second World War, then, America acquired control of more than half the world without its having to make a blood sacrifice worth mentioning in connection with such an operation.

Not even such unparalleled political successes fill the soul of the American People with satisfaction. America, as a People, is organic, and will forever remain isolationist. Isolationism is the only American characteristic that can be called "nationalism." The American soul does not delight at all in this world power. It finds in it no reason for pride. When in 1947 the Washington regime calmly handed over China to Russia, that is, the focus of America's quarter of the world's power, Americans took no notice. The diplomatic intermediary in the transfer was publicly honored and draped with medals. Only a few years after the War, ships were taken from the American fleet and delivered to Japan en masse to serve as the basis of a new Japanese navy. No American nationalist protested, for in America there are no nationalists, only victimized isolationists.

It is a strange phenomenon, and History will deal with it as with so many other transient paradoxes, that between the Second and Third World Wars American troops were stationed all along the perimeter of the political world, viz., the northeast quadrant of the planet, and this wide dispersion of American armed forces did not involve any kind of national exultation for Americans. The reason for that is Americans are primarily economics-oriented. The Masculine Principle is to realize higher ideas through art, warfare, Politics. Nothing could be further from the American ideal than that. The Feminine Principle is to nourish and preserve life - that is the American ideal. Americans therefore do not delight in an "empire" that continually lays claim to their wealth and constantly demands a reduction in their standard-of-living. In its traditional isolation, America needed no armies, garrisons, subventions to foreign countries, and Great Wars. The superficial politization of America has brought the American People economic injuries, and thus confirmed it in its isolation.

The American casualty lists in the first two World Wars, slight as they were numerically, hit the American People in a sensitive spot. No mother rejoices in the death of her children, and matriarchy informs the American soul. Americans do not love their victories, whereas the deaths they count bitterly. Long before American intervention in each of the two World Wars, there was already a de facto state-of-war between America and European or Asiatic belligerents. In each case, the possession of numerous "allies" provided Americans with a certain solace. In the Second World War, long lists of American allies were published, and considered effective propaganda even though few of the "allies" were still power-factors or even existed. Indeed, with the alternative: war now with allies, or war later, standing alone, America can be forced into a war. The old European proverb: Viel' Feind, viel' Ehr finds no resonance in matriarchal America.

This American character-trait is a Ponderable of which Europe must take account in shaping its policy. In the American mind (and likewise in the policy-decisions of the Culturally-alien Washington regime), Europe is the basis of every war-plan against Russia. This Ponderable might be used by Europe in either one or the other of two ways, as will be shown later. Moreover, Europe's Culture-bearing stratum must keep in mind that it does not matter at this time whether America, as a People, can regain its independence and sovereignty or whether it will remain simply the instrumental part of the Symbiosis America-Jewry. For political purposes, America and Jewry have become a unit; what name this unit receives is not important.

It remains for us to compare and evaluate from a political standpoint the psychology of the two extra-European powers, America-Jewry and Russia.

THE CONCERT OF BOLSHEVISM

Neither Russia nor America-Jewry belongs to the Western Civilization, though America, considered abstractly in and of itself, as it was before the Revolution of 1933, is still a European colonial-people.

Hence there is no Cultural casus belli in the coming Third World War between these two powers. They both belong to the Outer Revolt against the world-supremacy of the West, and the collective term for this revolt, which turns, destroying and negating, against the creative affirmation of the Western Destiny, is Bolshevism. Within the Concert of Bolshevism there are, of course, differences as well as similarities. Both must be evaluated.

With both world-powers, the reigning ideology comes from a bygone Western world-outlook. The American ideology of "freedom," "equality," and legalism stems from 18th century Europe, as does its underlying philosophy of materialism. The Russian ideology of Marxism comes from 19th century English Capitalism, of which Marxism is a supplement. In Russia, Marxism is treated as a religion, for the prime characteristic of the Russian soul is its religiosity. Whatever this soul takes seriously, be it even the absurd end-product of Western materialism – Pavlovian reflexology, scientific psychology -, it deals with in a religious way, that is, in a way transcending action. Nowhere in Russian life is there anything that in any way corresponds to the Marxist schema. The Russian soul is not yet politically mature, and Russia continues to use Marxism as a political export article, even though a market for it no longer exists, since the First World War buried the form-world of the 19th century for ever. America-Jewry, which is similarly maladapted to the New Age, exports to Europe the shop-worn ideology of Montesquieu, Constant, Mill, Bentham, and hopes that on this basis it can turn the Destiny of Europe back two centuries.

In America, on the other hand, Marxism is not a theory but a fact. In the realm of facts, Marxism means class-war. America is the classic land of finance-capitalism and trade unions, the two organized groups that systematically plunder the national economy. Not only Marx, but all 19th century theorizers were obsessed with economic doctrines - Malthus, Darwin, Mill, Spencer, Shaw. American life is essentially oriented to economics, and every aspect of Life is simply referred for its justification thereto.

Feminine-matriarchal life is routine; hence American life is routine and technicised. Books instruct the population "How To Win Friends," how social life, family life, sexual life are to be conducted. Yet this uniformization of life is not perceived as burdensome or ignominious the American population is entirely passive and feels quite at home in this atmosphere of a nursery. The social instincts predominate over the individual instincts, and every American child is taught from his earliest days that the essence of leading a successful life consists in "getting along with people." There is no other way to realize this ideal than to renounce one's individuality. That is the explanation for the difficulty of kindling any kind of political opposition in America. As soon as a policy secures a foothold and becomes popular, it is right and respectable. Radical or persistent criticism is impossible in America; the term "individualist" is nearly an insult. The extirpation of strong individuality precludes the rise of a true elite, an aristocracy, a ruling-stratum, for these are always based upon strong individuality and the feeling of uniqueness. All feelings of superiority, of higher self-esteem, of uniqueness are educated out of the American while he is still in kindergarten. It is impressed on him that his existence, his problems are exactly like those of everybody else.

An elementary demand of Life, however, is that every group possess a stratified social articulation. America's "elite" for economic, technical, industrial, social purpose is the business class, those thirty thousand technical-managerial brains that permit American life to function. For political purposes, the "elite" is the Jewish entity, which enjoys a monopoly of power in all matters but is especially conspicuous in the direction of foreign affairs. The technical-managerial caste has no sense of carrying out a mission; it does not regard itself as superior in nature, but only as more proficient in intellectual-technical matters. This type of social-technical differentiation resembles that which exists among the social insects, for example, the bees and ants.

Russian life is fundamentally barbarian. The barbarian is to be distinguished not only from Culture-men, but from savages, primitives, fellaheen, and decadents as well. Barbarian is a word full of promise, for the barbarian is inwardly in motion. The Germanic tribes that occupied Imperial Rome were barbarians, and from this Germanic stock came, many centuries later, men who wrought the Western Culture. The barbarian is the pre-Cultural form of humanity, just as different from the fellah, the end-product of a Culture, as from the savage, the proto-human type that stands in no relation whatever to a High Culture. The barbarian is strong willed yet irresolute. He can be readily converted to new doctrines – witness the Russian "conversion" to Marxism -, but the conversion must be superficial, for mere verbiage cannot abolish the difference between Culture-man and barbarian. The barbarian is rough and tough, not keen witted, full of artifice, and certainly not legalistic and intellectualized. He is the opposite of decadent. He is ruthless and does not shrink back from destroying what others may prize highly.

America's ideology - 18th century materialistic egalitarianism and 19th century capitalism - and Russia's ideology - 19th century proletarian capitalism - are both permeated with the spirit of their respective populations, the American ideology with that of the amalgam of negro-Jewish-Asiatic-Indian-European elements, as modified by the peculiarities of the landscape, the Russian ideology with that of the nomadic tribes of Asia, which are imbued with the enormous impersonality of the Asiatic steppes.

The Culture-man outside the Culture-sphere stands in danger of losing his Cultural-orientation - what the British civil administration in India used to call "going negative." During the expansion of the American population over the vast plains, the American colonial lost well-nigh every contact with Western tradition and Western happenings, and his Western culture was diluted. Only in one part of America was there a successful transplantation of Western culture, in the South, but it was destroyed, for all practical purposes, by the victory of the Yankees in the Secession War, 1861-1865. While the American lost his Western culture, step by step, he became primitive. Had he fought a Culturally-alien world, such as the Chinese or Hindu, he would have retained his Cultural-orientation in fullest measure, for conflict with the Alien strengthens the Proper. But he fought merely savages and, more often, the landscape itself, the hardships of Nature. In the inward contest between Culture and Landscape, Landscape was largely the victor. Because comfort is one of the main ideals of the American, his vital impetus finds expression primarily in the domain of technics. Unrestrained by tradition, by political or social considerations, he fell head over heels into absolute technical development, and - in technics - he made his the foremost among the Western Colonies. Thus, as a result of his century of stateless expansion, the American succumbed; on the one hand, to the primitivity of his vast and empty continent, while, as a result of the concentration made possible for him by the absence of power-struggles, on the other, he made himself in some respects superior to Europeans. This had as its consequence yet another peculiarity.

The simultaneous presence of primitivity and over-civilization in the American shaped his relationship to Europe into an unhealthy one. With his strong technical aptitude, he came to regard Europe as inferior; with his primitivity, he failed to comprehend Europe's Cultural Imperative in the 20th century. Hence he offered no resistance when the Culture-distorting regime foisted on America the idea that it had to educate Europe.

This idea could be all the more inculcated since America is by nature feminine-matriarchal and attributes great value to formal education. In America the autodidact will find neither political, academic, professional, nor social recognition. This peculiarity of the American character has been aggravated by the Culture distorting element, and American schools and universities have been made into scholastic factories that produce uniform biological units. They have eradicated human individuality, so far as that can be attained at all in the human species. All values imparted through this "education," such as comfort, security, and social uniformity, may be found on the purely animal level in man. None appeal to the specifically human level, which is embodied at highest potential by the unique and individualized human being, with his loftier values.

While the American is a Culture-man, *reprimitivised* on the one side of his being, over-civilized on the other, since he is completely and entirely animated by the ideals of peace, comfort, and security, the Russian is a barbarian, and still wholly primitive. Centuries of Petrinism never touched the underground Russia. No matter that it figured as such for centuries, Russia never became a nation of the West. America is a genuine Western colony, though, to be sure, it must now be counted part of the Outer Revolt.

The orientation towards technics is common to both: America is technical by instinct; Russia has become so under compulsion from its leaders, who have only politico-military reasons for embracing technics. In the field of philosophy, America's sole contribution to the Western intellectual heritage was Pragmatism - the doctrine that Truth is "what works." In other words, Truth is not a function of the Soul, but of Nature. Pragmatism is at once a primitive and over-civilized philosophy, primitive, because its position vis-à-vis Truth is devoid of higher culture; over-civilized, because it makes all Truth merely an attribute of Technics. Expressed in terms of the American psychology: "True is what procures me more security, more comfort." In America, obsession with technics is the expression and content of life of the population. It is instinctive, and America naturally seeks to export it to whatever countries its armies and bomber-squadrons have conquered. In Russia, on the other hand, the technics-obsession merely serves political and military ends, and is imposed on the Russian population only through the apparatus of a political dictatorship. The Russian experiences things primarily in a religious way; hence the incredible spectacle of his worshipping a machine.

Russia exhibits the same education-obsession as America: In the words of Lunacharsky: "Education, distributed according to

Marxist principles, can make even the most mediocre Oriental intelligent." Once again, a common denominator with America. There, too, "intelligence" is regarded as something that can be acquired, and, moreover, as the only distinction between human beings. Both Russia and America hold that the External forms and conditions the mind. Both emphasize totally environment and experience, negate dogmatically Spirit and Soul. For both the collective man is the ideal and the prevalent type. In both there naturally exists the most extreme intolerance towards anything other than the mass-ideal.

In Russia, the craze for uniformity, including the education mania, is likewise imposed from above to carry out a political program. The emphasis on the power of environment, the adoration of reflexology, the idolization of machines, of statistics and percentages, and of economic theories generally - all this is in Russia simply technique, and it is all essentially negative: the Russian peasant-barbarian soul is a religious ferment, and, as such, abhors economic theories, machines, science, and nationalism. The program of Moscow-Bolshevism represents a means of quashing the hyper-individuality of a people of Pugachevs, Aksakovs, Kropotkins, Nechayevs, Dostoievskys, Rasputins, and Shoptsy. Primarily, Moscow-Bolshevism is a method for politicizing the religious-barbarian Russia. That the Moscow regime uses Marxism as an export-article is simply political idiocy, and the possibility constantly exists that it will one day discard it because of its ineffectiveness.

For Europe the following distinction is important: American-Jewish Bolshevism is the instinctive destruction of the West through primitive, anti-Cultural ideas - peace, comfort, security, abolition of individuality -, through over-technicization, through the imposition of Culture-distortion and Culture-retardation. Russian Bolshevism seeks to attain the destruction of the West in the spirit of pan-Slavic religiosity, i.e., the Russification of all humanity.

Thus American-Jewish Bolshevism poses a real spiritual threat to Europe. In its every aspect, American-Jewish Bolshevism strikes a weak spot in the European organism. Even in Europe there exists a stratum, the Michel-stratum, the inner-America, which is animated by the purely animal American ideal of peace, comfort, security, abolition of individuality. Even in Europe there is an element that would like to replace culture with machinery. Even on Europe Culture-retarding regimes can be imposed, if necessary with American bayonets. Even in Europe Culture-distortion is present: the dictature over Europe of the American-Jewish Symbiosis itself. And even in Europe, in the midst of the Age of Absolute Politics, the Cato-type exists: You can watch him babbling, misty-eyed, about democratic ideals while the Barbarian and the Distorter occupy the sacred soil of the West. The 20th century European Cato would rather see the West destroyed than have finally to toss the rubbish of democratic ideals on the scrap heap of history, where the corpse of Democracy lies stinking and putrescent after a half century of decay.

Russian Bolshevism is simply barbarism, and therefore finds no resonance anywhere in Europe. Even Europe's lowest spiritual stratum, the inner traitor, the Michel-stratum, has nothing whatever in common with the pan-Slavism of barbaric population-streams. Russian religiosity has been temporarily and, from a Cultural standpoint, falsely raised to political intensity as a reflex of the great Western spiritual development, the Resurgence of Authority, the genesis of the Imperium-Idea. Without the Western Culture, there would be no such structure as Russia, only marauding tribes of barbaric horsemen like the Cossacks in Taras Bulba.

Russian Bolshevism is therefore less dangerous to Europe than American-Jewish Bolshevism, for no aspect of its menace corresponds to a weakness in Europe's spiritual armor. Europe actually has an inner America, the Michel-stratum; however, Europe has no inner Russia. Obviously, the so-called Communist Parties are not at all the reliable tools wherewith a Russian occupation of Europe could be built. In fact, the work of these Communist Parties is already done. They were useful instruments of early Bolshevism's foreign policy, especially in the period 1933-1939. During the Second World War, they helped save Russia's existence as a political unit; after the War, they helped create the Russian power-accumulation, extending from Hanover to Hong-Kong, the largest contiguous power accumulation in the history of the world. Yet, today, between the Second and Third World Wars, all Communist Parties, including the American, are politically insignificant.

The Communist Parties of the West are simply class-war units, not bearers of barbarism and Russian pan-Slav nationalism. In the 20th century, all are forced to think in terms of facts and not merely words, so far as Politics is concerned, and Russia's connection with Western class-war rests simply on words. Russia claims to be the bearer of class war in the West. Nevertheless, during the Second World War the Moscow regime forbade the American Communist Party to engage in class-warfare. Actually, the entire policy of using Marxism as a political export-article is now political stupidity, for Marxism has lost its former rabble-rousing value in the West. The highpoint of class-war in the West has passed.

In particular, it was the re-orientation of Russian world-policy after the Second World War, the turning against the Jewish entity of

Church-State-Nation-People-Race, that sealed the doom of every Communist Party in the West, the one in America included.

The blow that the American-Jewish Symbiosis has dealt the European organism is well-known. The values of this Symbiosis are purely animal, anti-Spiritual, anti-Aristocratic, anti-Cultural, anti-Heroic, anti-Imperialist, and therefore appeal to the worst element in the European population and to the worst in every individual European. In each point of its attack, America-Jewry opposes the values of Capitalism to those of Imperialism, the heroic world-outlook of the Age of Absolute Politics. With the spiritual-ethical values of Capitalism, America-Jewry is planning to kill the Western organism. But since the Past can never destroy the Future, only attempt to thwart it, that means American bayonets imposing the anti-Cultural Interregnum on Europe, and therein lies the possibility that for Europe will follow many decades of degradation, chaos, darkness, stultification, misery, and wasting away.

The effect that a Russian occupation of Europe would have on the Western Culture is not yet equally well-known, and can be determined only by uncovering its organic basis.

The Russian is a barbarian; the European is a Culture-man in his late-Civilization phase. Before this moment in History, barbarians have violently invaded Culture-areas. In the 16th century B.C., Northern barbarians invaded the Egyptian Culture-petrifact, to enact the chapter of history that is called the "Hyksos"-era. About 1700 B.C., the Kassites conquered and occupied the Babylonian Culture-area, and, around the same time, the Aryans in a barbaric wave from the North flooded into and conquered the Culture of the Indus. Chinese history in its first stirrings is the epic of a barbarian invasion by the Chou. Imperial Rome – even Republican Rome - was invaded more than once by the barbarian Germans and Gauls. In none of these historical instances did the invasion of the barbarians destroy the body of the Culture; in each case the result was finally the absorption of the barbarian elements into the Culture-body or their expulsion. The barbarian comes to destroy and stays to learn. Spiritually, the barbarian is a tabula rasa. Labile and childlike, he is eager to apply the new doctrines, new life-forms, to which he has been converted. Hence the Romanov Petersburg of the 18th and 19th centuries displayed a higher degree of Western Politesse and social-form than any European capital before it.

The belief that a Russian-barbarian occupation of the whole of Europe would be similar to the Russian occupation of half of Germany after the Second World War is a completely false estimate of the possibilities. A Russian occupation of all Europe would involve an entirely different distribution of forces and a completely different psychological situation. In the first place, the Russian occupation after the Second World War originated as a gift from America. Cynically, Europe's border against Asia, which had been pushed back gradually over a millennium, was restored to its place of 900 years ago. Thus the history, honor, and traditions of thirty generations of Europeans were outraged. The atrocities committed during the first years of the Russian occupation were permitted, encouraged, and even imitated by America. Without American encouragement, Russia would not have been in the position to commit its atrocities. In the second place, Europe was not politically able to intervene to protect 30,000,000 Europeans, for every European country was governed by the Churchill-regimes the Americans had appointed, and these puppet-governments greeted barbarian Russia as their "valiant ally" while their members exchanged decorations with those of the Moscow regime.

Russia's occupation of a small part of Europe and its domination over one tenth of the European population after the Second World War were made possible only by the Washington regime, which, in 1945, wanted Europe so divided that the Red Flag would wave over Berlin and Vienna. If the Washington regime, instead of giving Russia simply a small part of Europe, had abandoned to it all of Europe - and that is a possibility contained in the events to come -, the division of forces would be completely different. Instead of America Jewry, the whole of Russia, Eastern Europe, and most of Western Europe - under Churchill-regimes - ranged against part of Germany, then against 200,000,000 Russians, would be arrayed the total body of the West, 250,000,000 men who are superior to them in intelligence, technical skill, organizational talent, and will-to-power. If this happens, America will be expelled from Europe, once and for all. Europe will have but a single enemy. That would be a unifying factor such as did not exist from the First Crusade until Lepanto.

A Russian occupation would develop along one or the other of two lines. The first possibility is an endless series of European uprisings against Russia that could result only in the expulsion of the demoralized barbarians. The second possibility would result from Russia's introducing a clever regime and according Europe extensive autonomy and magnanimous treatment. Within a few decades, this Europe would naturally aim at infiltrating horizontally the whole Russian seat of origin, its technical, economic, social, and finally, military and political life. Instead of the Russification of Europe, as Dostoievsky and Aksakov dreamt of it, would result the Europeanization of Russia once again, and this time in far stronger degree. This would occur from pure historical necessity, since this is the Age of Absolute Politics and Europe is politically shrewd whereas barbarian Russia is formless and politically inept, fluctuating between senseless vehemence and inner doubt. Not even the most brilliant statesmen in Russia could use this barbarian material to subjugate Europe in this Imperialist stage of its Destiny. An attempt by Russia to integrate Europe into its power-accumulation peacefully would eventually result in the rise of a new Symbiosis: Europe-Russia. Its final form would be that of a European Imperium. An attempt by Russia to chastise and terrorize Europe without the help of America would result in Russia's expulsion from Europe for good, by a Europe whose own dormant barbarian instincts had been thus reawakened.

If Russia should occupy Europe and attempt to imitate the American policy of encouraging petty-stateism, to divide and conquer, it would fail utterly. America has been successful in that policy only because of its access to the European Michel-stratum with its lickspittle Churchill's. The Michel yearns for American capitalism and liberalism, but trembles with abysmal cowardice before Russian barbarism. The Communist Parties would be of slight use to Russia in any attempt to set up puppet governments on the model of America's Churchill regimes. The leadership and membership of these Communist Parties is composed of inferior European types, not of pan-Slavs or religious Russian nationalists. The barbarian, immature and unversed in the subtleties of the art of Politics, trusts only those who are of his own religion, and the true religion of the Russian is not Marxism, but Russia. The first victims of a Russian occupation of Europe would be the European Communists, who would be liquidated at the slightest suspicion of disloyalty. Their "Communism" stems from books, their pro-Russian sentiments from hatred and envy of their European surroundings, their utopian orthodoxy about Russia comes from a lack of realism and an exaggerated intellectualism. The Russian knout and the Russian revolver would soon teach them what they have not learnt from their books, would shatter their utopian ideals and give their hatred a new focus.

Russia's effect on petty-stateism and petty-nationalism would in no way resemble America's successful perpetuation of these Culture-pathological phenomena. To carry out its policy in Europe, America needs petty-stateism. Not only does it work in the spirit of the principle, divide et impera, it also cannot think outside the narrow framework of it. After the Second World War, the Washington regime, which held absolute power to force its will on enfeebled Europe, announced its policy of a "united Europe." It then proceeded to Balkanize Europe politically and atomize it socially in unparalleled fashion. Numerous congresses of toothless and infantile old men from the 19th century passed even more numerous resolutions, but the result was continued disunity and chaos. The childish dotards had received permission from Washington to jabber about the "unification" of Europe as much as they liked, but they were not allowed to say a word about the Liberation of Europe. That is why all these congresses led to nothing. For the Unification of Europe and the Liberation of Europe are one and the same process: seen from within, it is Unification; from without, liberation.

The fact that Russia used the fiction of "independent" states in its post-War occupation of Eastern Europe offers no criterion for its policy in the event it should occupy Western Europe, the Europe that is synonymous with the Western Culture. In any case, simply the presence of the barbarian, let alone his policy, would dissolve the Inner Enemy of Europe, the Michel-stratum, and thus liberate all creative forces within Europe from the tyranny of the Past.

Without the Michel, without his leaders, namely the Churchill's, without American bayonets, the distribution of forces would be as follows: the European will-to-power and the European Destiny against the sheer military might of a barbarian horde. The dissolution of the Michel-stratum would automatically destroy petty-stateism, for petty-statist ideals and theories are preserved only in Culture-retarding brains. The barbarian, whether he wished it or not, would complete the spiritual unification of Europe by removing the only inner-European obstacle to that unity. From the Spiritual to the Political is but one step.

The following would be the results of the two possible kinds of Russian policy, the far-sighted policy of striving to integrate Europe into an enormous Russian Empire, embracing the whole world, and the policy of attempting to rule Europe by terror and violence.

Should Russia aim at a lasting incorporation of Europe into its Empire, it could succeed only if it granted Europe significant concessions. The first of these would have to be administrative autonomy for Europe as a unit, for that is the desire of all Europeans - the Michel-stratum and its leaders, the senile Churchill's, of course, accepted.

Should Russia attempt to terrorize Europe, it would summon forth in the European People the will to counter-terror. Faced with the barbarian, all Europeans, even the simplest minded liberals, would learn the necessity of inner firmness, of a stern will, the virtues of Command and Obedience, for these alone could force the barbarian to accept demands, or else retreat to his tundra's and steppes. All Europeans would realize that not parliamentary babble, class-war, capitalism, and elections, but only Authority, the Will-to-Power, and finally, the military spirit could ever drive out the barbarian. The expulsion of England's army of 40,000 men by a few hundred Irish guerrilla-fighters in the years 1916-1923 would be repeated on a larger scale. In a great, unrelenting War of Liberation, Europe would unite itself, and cast the barbarian back to the distant plains of Asia.

To conclude: Between the two powers in the Concert of Bolshevism that dominates this Second Interbellum-Period, there are numerous similarities, some profound, others superficial. Neither of :he two is an organism with a positive Mission; neither of the two exhibits the inner qualities that alone can found and preserve a world system; neither of them has or can have an aristocracy; in short, neither of them is the seat of a High Culture. In both the element of Landscape predominates over the cultural component in every stratum of the human material; both make use of an antiquated Western ideology that is completely ineffectual in the world-situation of the Age of Absolute Politics; both have not the faintest inkling of the Imperium-Idea, the necessary fulfillment whereof is the total historical meaning of this Age; both believe it possible to attain a static world-order in which History would have ceased to exist, and this belief makes both dangerously relentless; both believe Europe can be destroyed as a politico-Cultural unit, and degraded to the level of China.

Thus, from the European standpoint, there is in a Cultural sense no choice between these two powers, for both represent fundamental opposites to European Cultural imperatives. In their political relation to Europe, however, the two extra-European powers widely and fundamentally differ. Owing to the presence of a European inner America, the Washington regime is able to establish or maintain in every European country: Culture-distortion, petty-stateism, finance-capitalism, democracy, economic distress, and chaos. Regardless of its intentions, Russia produces a spiritual aversion throughout Europe. If America, deliberately or otherwise, relinquished to Russia the whole of Europe, Russia's occupation would have to be based either on terror or large-scale concessions to procure collaboration. Both occupation policies would end in the domination of Russia by Europe, either through a peaceful inner conquest or a series of Liberation Wars that Europe would wage as a unit against Russia. Barbarian Russia can only awaken Europe's sterner instincts. The American-Jewish Symbiosis, composed of fellah-Jews and American colonials who are at once primitive and over-civilized, appeals to the lowest stratum of Europe and to the lowest stratum in every European, the stratum of animal instincts, laziness, cowardice, avarice, dishonor, and ethical individualism. America can only divide Europe-no matter what its policy. Russia can only unite Europe-no matter what its policy.

From their comparative relationships to Europe, it follows quite clearly that a Russian-barbarian domination of all Europe, if such a thing were brought about by American policy-and that is the only way such an event could occur-would be less injurious to the Destiny of Europe than a continuation of the American-Jewish domination, for the barbarian, by his very presence, would dissolve the Inner Enemy of Europe, the Michel-stratum, and unite Europe spiritually.

This brings us to the concrete question of political decisions for Europe. The political question would be: How is power to be enlarged? But since Europe has no power, the question is: How is power to be obtained? There are only two political units in the world; hence the question is simply: From which political unit can Europe wrest away power? Or in other words: Who is the Enemy?

THE POLITICAL ENEMY OF EUROPE

The armistice that concluded the Second World War left Europe divided between Russia and America-Jewry. Russia received ten per cent of Europe's population; America-Jewry was allotted ninety per cent. By Europe is meant here, of course, the Cultural Europe, viz., Germany, France, England, Italy, Spain, together with tiny provinces like Switzerland, and not the geographic "Europe" that is an historically worthless concept.

The Washington regime naturally seeks to convince its European subjects to identify the interests of America-Jewry with their own and therefore prepare Europe for war against Russia in alliance with it. The propaganda that aims at enlisting Europe's participation in this war has three main points: first, Russia is not a "democracy"; second, it "enslaves" other peoples; third, a Russian occupation of Europe would result in the slaughter of the whole European population or a considerable part thereof.

The first point is politically meaningless, nor is the second point worth taking seriously. To enslave two hundred and fifty million people who are spiritually, ethically, scientifically, technically, militarily, and politically the most highly developed in the world is impossible. So far as Europeans can be enslaved at all, they are already enslaved by America-Jewry. Today the people of Europe work with every possible exertion for the enrichment and aggrandizement of the financiers, industrial barons, politicians, and generals of North America. Slavery no longer means the rattling of chains, rather shortages of currency and materials, rationing, unemployment, occupation soldiers and their families, puppet-governments, rearmament and military programs on a gigantic scale.

The third point seeks to frighten Europeans into a war to destroy America-Jewry's sole dynamic opponent, thus placing the masters of New York and Washington in control of the entire world. But again, to kill a considerable part of the European population through short-term violent measures would be impossible. The well-planned and systematically executed starvation of Germany by the American-Jewish occupation during the period 1945-1948 killed approximately 3,000,000 people. That is probably the largest number of people that could have been killed by such methods. Overheated brains that could be persuaded that Europe "killed 6,000,000 Jews" can readily imagine the course a Russian massacre of hundreds of millions of human beings would take. People who believe in such nightmares lack a sense for exaggeration, and their psychology is entirely wanting. No great number of men can be trained to kill, directly and systematically, as a daily performance, from morning till evening, over an extended period, unarmed men, women, and children. Certainly, the mere sporadic killing of the kind involved in every military invasion could never reduce the population of Europe to any great extent.

If a selective killing should be the method in an attempt to behead the European organism, then Russia would be likewise incapable of that. This was the method of the American-Jewish "war-crimes" program, the most extensive terror in the history of the world. America-Jewry attempted to isolate the elite and string up its members one by one; but there, too, it missed the mark. Russia did not practice any systematic "war-crimes" terror, in spite of encouragement on the part of America-Jewry, since it was more interested in individuals as material for the Future than in settling past accounts according to Mosaic Law. Furthermore, the American Colonials and their exotic leaders understand much better than the barbarian how to go about isolating and exterminating superior individuals, for the inner structure and cohesion of the Western Culture are much less familiar to him and much less understood by him. A profound ignorance of the outside world goes hand in hand with Russian xenophobia.

America-Jewry insists that Russia could overwhelm Europe quite mechanically and automatically-were not American colonial troops here. Yet the fact remains that only America's intervention in the Second World War prevented Europe from destroying Russia as a political unit. The present Russian power-accumulation was thus created by America-Jewry. Never in the five centuries of Russian history has Russia been able to make way into Europe unless supported by one or more European states. Against Frederick the Great

Russia received aid from France, Austria, and Sweden; against Napoleon Russia received aid from England, Austria, Prussia, Sweden, and Spain. In 1945, .Russia penetrated into Germany only with America's assistance. Before American intervention, Europe had hurled the barbarian back across the Volga. Russia is a threat only to a divided Europe; a united Europe could destroy the power of Bolshevist Russia at the moment of its choosing. That Europe has need of America-Jewry to defend itself against Russia is a crass lie.

Only America can grant Russia entry into Europe; this was true in 1945, and will be just as true in 1967 or 1975. There are two ways in which America-Jewry could deliver Europe to a Russian-Bolshevist occupation: by voluntarily making Russia a gift of it, as it did with China in 1947, or by losing a war against Russia from European bases.

In any case, Europe-that means here above all the Culture bearing stratum-will choose its own enemy because the 250,000 men who are mystically charged with fulfilling the Destiny of Europe are by nature inwardly free of Culturally alien influences. Enemy propaganda, however great its extent may be, cannot frustrate the Destiny of a High Culture, for that Destiny is above mechanism and technics, and propaganda is simply a technique. An enemy occupying Europe can probably round up herds of civilians by means of its puppet-governments and call the result an army, but beyond that it cannot go. An army means, first, morale; second, an officer-corps; third, a high command; and, fourth, the human material of the troops. A herd of civilians conscripted under foreign coercion would possess no morale and have no European officer-corps and European high command. Without these, they would be only an armed mob, and, as such, not a formidable match for the barbarians.

We have seen that it is a deep spiritual need of the matriarchal American People to have many and strong allies in a war; and of the ruling-stratum in America it must be remarked that the rider is always limited to the abilities of his mount. We have also seen that Europe is the basis for America's every war-plan against Russia. Europe may be able to exploit these facts.

To secure the collaboration of Europe in the war it is planning against Russia, America would grant Europe huge concessions--in inner autonomy, in commerce, in military affairs, and even in administrative unification. But since America has the Michel-stratum at its disposal, and this stratum holds office everywhere in Europe, no demands are put to it. Thus the Washington regime can treat Europeans as something less than peons-peons at least receive a wage. The Churchill's of every country make no demands lest they disquiet the American bayonets upon which their tenure of office depends. To expect pride and independence from the stratum of professional traitors is simply unrealistic.

The second way in which the American People's spiritual need to have allies might be exploited, would be through an unswerving, voluntary, neutralization of Europe vis-à-vis the projected war against Russia. Once the Washington regime was forced to accept European neutrality as a fact, it would have to abandon its plans for a European theatre-of-war and evacuate Europe.

Either of these possibilities, if realized, could bring about the Liberation of Europe before the Third World War. The first possibility could be realized only if the Michel-stratum were removed from public life, for the Churchill's would scarcely place Europe's interests above their class and personal interests, which are protected only by the foreign occupation.

To act creatively in Politics, one must begin with the right choice of enemy. If one selects an enemy from whom one can win no power, the end-result is suicide, as we saw with the self-destruction of the English Empire in the Second World War. Were Europe actually to fight for an enemy, that would be proof that Europe had in fact died, but the continuing mystical relation between the European Culture-bearing stratum and the European population would prevent Europe from doing so. Should the Third World War occur, Europe will participate in it only on its own terms. That is an absolute mystical certainty. Perhaps a herd of hapless conscripts without morale, without European officers and a European high command, can be thrown on the battlefield to fight for an enemy, but that would hardly be European participation worthy of the name.

All this has long since answered the question: Who is the Enemy? The enemy must be a political unit at whose expense we can gain power. America-Jewry has the power in Europe, and if Europe would win back its sovereignty, it can do so only at the expense of America-Jewry. Politics is concrete, and thus the argument that Russia wishes to conquer Europe has but little force. Perhaps India would like to do that as well, but Europe must reckon on facts and not on threats. America has the power in Europe, and, therefore, America is the Enemy.

Two facts dominate the politics of Europe in this historical period: Europe will never fight for its Enemy; Europe will survive the Third World War and its aftermath, regardless of the new weaponry.

These are metaphysical facts; they possess Destiny value and cannot be removed by human action. They correspond to all life-furthering, life-affirming, power-increasing instincts of the European People, to the super-personal Destiny of the Western Culture. In view of these facts, the enemy propaganda of the Russian bogey can be called simply idiotic. America-Jewry is the bearer of the Russian menace, today, as in the Second World War. If it brings about a Russian occupation of all Europe, then all Europe will persevere and overcome that happening. Should America be expelled from Europe before the Third World War, the form of the war would be completely different. Instead of America-Jewry versus Russia, it would then be the European Imperium versus Russia, and in that form the war would end in the destruction of Russia as a political unit. For the European Imperium, the result would be external security for the coming centuries. Should America attempt to intervene, as before, this time its efforts would be of no avail, for the European Imperium will naturally include England and Ireland. It was only America's fortuitous possession of those bases that enabled it to stab Europe in the back during the Second World War. From North America or Africa, America Jewry could do little or nothing to help Russia.

The Age is mighty and its tasks enormous, but if we hold fast to our honor and pride, harken to our own instincts and the Inner Imperative, we will win the upper hand in every instance. Although the opponents are gigantic, they are formless; behind their patchwork power accumulations is a spiritual void which, like a vacuum, will draw back their dispersed forces. Neither America-Jewry nor Russia is a structure inwardly adapted to the Age of Absolute Politics. The American People is matriarchal, isolationist, and interested only in economic matters. When the power-adventures at the antipodes run into too much money or demand real blood-sacrifice, the Washington regime will no longer be able to force it to tread the false path of senseless World Wars. In the World War, Germany lost 739 Generals, whereas America had the death of a single General to mourn. This fact just symbolizes the truth that America has enjoyed success without having to pay the price of it. The moment the adventures become too costly, the Washington regime will have to retreat, for even its "victories" mean nothing to the American People. An apolitical people cannot win an enduring political victory; it does not need it, or want it, or even know how it would use the power proceeding from it.

The Russian barbarian does not understand power; he has no knowledge of the meaning of this Age. Neither the half Westernized Bolshevists nor the pure-Asiatic masses possess the qualities needed to build an empire. The spiritually unadulterated Russian, whose limitations are binding for the Moscow regime, is religious, hence inward; he is rural and land-hungry, but there is no nobility and no religion in Russia that attend to his material and spiritual cares. Marxism is a collection of dead and sterile phrases, and can no more strongly inspire the Russian than it can the European. Pan-Slav religiosity does not seek an empire; with it an empire cannot be built.

This is the Age of Absolute Politics, and its meaning is the fulfillment of the Destiny of the Western Civilization: the formation of the European Imperium and the actualization of its World-Mission. In this Age, a power that would impose its will on the world must be endowed with the inner qualities that alone can establish and maintain a world-system, the qualities of the Spanish Europe in the 16th century, the English Europe in the 18th and 19th centuries, the Prussian Ethical Socialist Europe in the 20th century, which will survive the 21st century. The one, great, all-embracing quality that is absolutely necessary for such a task is the consciousness of a Mission. That cannot come from human resolves; it can come only as the emanation of a super-personal soul, the organ of a higher Destiny, a Divinity. The American-Jewish and Russian ideas of negative world-conquest are but vague caricatures of the true, Western European Idea of Imperium Mundi, a travesty of History on the world-stage.

Europe recognizes its Cultural enemies and its sole political enemy. Thus it sees the only path it can follow. The basis of Europe's politics is faith in but under no circumstances fear of the Future. If we follow now the path that our instincts, our intelligence, and our Inner Imperative have prescribed, whatever befalls us shall be good. For us there is but one crime, one misdemeanor, and one mistake: that is to be untrue to ourselves and follow alien leaders and hold alien ideals.

Europe also recognizes its Inner Enemy: Whosoever pursues another policy than that of a sovereign Europe, whether this is the policy of America-Jewry or Russia, is the Inner Enemy. Petty-statists and petty-nationalists sink to the level of spies and foreign agents. Loyalty to Europe excludes every other political loyalty. No European owes the petty-state of his birth any allegiance whatever, for all these tiny erstwhile-states are now simply anti-European tools in the hands of our Enemy, the Washington regime.

Europe is equal to its historic task. Against the anti-spiritual, antiheroic "ideals" of America-Jewry, Europe pits its metaphysical ideas, its faith in its Destiny, its ethical principles, its heroism. Fearlessly, Europe falls in for battle, knowing it is armed with the mightiest weapon ever forged by History: the super-personal Destiny of the European organism. Our European Mission is to create the Culture-State-Nation-Imperium of the West, and thereby we shall perform such deeds, accomplish such works, and so transform our world that our distant posterity, when they behold the remains of our buildings and ramparts, will tell their grandchildren that on the soil of Europe once dwelt a tribe of gods.

THE DESTINY OF AMERICA

By *Francis P. Yockey*

Published January 1955

The early American arrived at a land of which he knew nothing. He did not know its geography, its fertility, its climate, its dangers. In the North, he encountered forests, rocky soil, and winters of a rigor he had not known before. In the South, he met with swamps, malaria, and dense forests. Everywhere he encountered the hostile savage with his scalping knife and his warfare against women and children. In little groups, these early Americans cleared the forests, and built homes and forts. The men plowed the fields with rifles slung over their shoulders, and in the house, the wife went about her duties with a loaded weapon near at hand. There were ships to and from Europe, and the colonials could have left their hardships and gone back -- but they would not admit defeat.

Out of these colonials was bred the Minute Man. Minute Man! These American farmers were ready at a minute's notice to abandon the plow and seize the gun. They knew that the hour of their political independence was at hand and instinctively they prepared for it. When the moment arrived, with a British order to arrest two of their leaders, the Minute Men assembled before daybreak at Lexington to face the British force sent to seize them. Though heavily outnumbered they stood their ground in the face of Major Pitcairn's order to disperse. "If they mean to have a war," said Captain John Parker, leader of the Minute Men, "let it begin here!"

Begin it did, and for 8 long years it continued. Concord, Bunker Hill, Boston, Ticonderoga, Quebec, New York, Long Island, Harlem Heights, White Plains, Fort Lee, Fort Washington, Valley Forge, Trenton, Princeton, Brandywine, Saratoga, Stony Point, Savannah, Camden, The Cowpens, Yorktown -- these names recall at once the terrific odds against which the colonials fought, the low points to which their fortunes reached, and the silent and steadfast devotion of the troops. At Valley Forge, the men were but half-clad, and rations, when there was food issued at all, were slim. Sickness was rife, and mortality was high, yet no one thought of surrender. General Washington said of them: "Naked and starving as they are we cannot enough admire the incomparable patience and fidelity of our soldiery."

No nation has produced individual soldiers to excel Nathaniel Greene, General Know, General Sullivan, John Stark, Nicholas Herkimer, Anthony Wayne, Daniel Morgan, John Paul Jones, nor greater patriots than John Dickinson, Richard Henry Lee, John Adams,

Benjamin Franklin, John Rutledge. These are but a few. The spirit which animated these heroes is part of the white race, and it will last while this race lasts. It waits for its reawakening upon the coming of great events to American soil once more. When the fields of this continent are visited once again by the stern creativeness of war -- war for the independence and the liberation of the pristine American colonial spirit -- the world shall see that Americans are not the weak-willed, self-interested, pleasure-mad morons that Hollywood has tried so desperately to make them.

It was the individual imperialism of the frontiersman-type that actually opened up and conquered the North American continent. Explorers like George Rogers Clark and John Fremont preceded the frontiersman into the wilderness, and he followed into the hostile land with its lurking warlike savages. With slung rifle he took wife and children and all his earthly belongings into the land ahead, unknown, unsettled, unplowed. Daily he surmounted a thousand dangers; he lived in the face of Death. This intrepid type who was at once explorer, warrior, minister, doctor, judge, and settler, advanced until he reached the Pacific, and then he looked toward Alaska and the westward islands.

The tragic defeat of the Federalists by the less worthy among the post-Revolution generation made it possible for sectionalism to arise in America, and out of sectionalism issued the disastrous "War Between the States." That war proved only that the heroic type of American occurred everywhere in this broad land. The only lesson we can learn from the sacrifice is that big-mouthed agitators of the vicious stamp of Theodore Parker and Horace Greeley are capable of consigning nations to the flames in order to actualize their fantastic egalitarian theories.

During the conquest of the continent, small carping voices were continually raised against the heroic performance. Congressmen laughed at the idea of governing a region so far away as the distant Pacific coast. The Poets Lowell and Whittier and the agitators Garrison and Phillips did their best to bring about a sectional war during all of the 40's and 50's. Calhoun's attempt to annex Texas was defeated by the Congress. Small minds were against the Mexican War and the acquisition of the Southwest. They opposed the acquisition of Hawaii, of the Philippines, of the Cuban protectorate. After the War Between the States, this type of mind, represented by men like Summer and Stevens, wanted to treat the Southerners as an alien and inferior people and to gloat over them while placing the conqueror's foot on their necks.

This type of mentality still survives in America. Today it still fights against greatness and heroism. Today it teaches the doctrine of liberalism with its pacifism, its love for the inferior and misbegotten, its internationalism which makes a virtue of treason, its hatred of all who possess strong national feelings, its toothless desire for racial equality, and its tolerance of everything and everyone, particularly the alien and the unfit. Today this type of mind -- namely, all those to whom liberal doctrines appeal -- are working for the anti-American forces, whether consciously or not. The sub-Americans are in the service of America's inner enemy.

We have seen the spirit of the white race: the spirit of divine discontent and self-help, the spirit of self-reliance, of fearlessness in the face of great danger, the feeling of racial superiority, the urge to great distances and the will to conquer all that lies between, the spirit of the Alamo. To the true American, his is a living, organic, white nation, and not a set of principles, of "four freedoms" or a "world-policeman". Of this feeling was every great American: Washington, Hamilton, Henry Clay, Robert E. Lee, Sam Houston. The American soldier shows in every war that even today this true American type survives.

But today the true Americans, the former great leaders, have been displaced by Morganthaus, Ezekiels, Paswolskis, Cohens, Frankfurters, Goldsmiths, Lubins, Berles, Schenks, Edelsteins, Baruchs, Goldwyns, Mayers, Strausses, Lilienthals, Hillmans, Rosenmans, Lehmanns, Rosenbergs, Eisenhowers.

We know the true American and we know the liberal -- the sub-type within the white race. Let us now look at the third group which came here only yesterday and which today is linked with the liberals, the internationalists, the class-warriors, the subverters, of America's white, European traditions. This group makes use of American slogans and American ideas, but that cannot conceal its alien provenance. Let us measure the significance of the newcomers and examine their history.

THE HISTORY OF THE JEW

The culture which produced the Jewish nation arose in Asia Minor around 100 B.C. This culture produced many nations, all of them, so far as we are concerned, similar to the Jews. These "nations" were not nations at all in our sense of the word, for they had no homeland. Citizenship in this alien type of nation was gained by being a believer in the religion of the group. Jews, Marcionites, Gnostics, Mohammedans -- all these were nations, and to all of them membership in the nation was gained by being a believer.

Intermarriage with non-believers was forbidden, and this inbreeding for two thousand years has made it possible today to pick out the Jew by his countenance. Thus, for the Jew, race and religion became identical, and if the Jew loses his religion, he loses little for he still remains a Jew by race. The unity of the race is not destroyed even though the great masses of the Jews become atheists.

After the dispersion of the Jews throughout Europe and Russia, they were entirely cut off from any contact with nations similar to themselves. They shut themselves up in the ghettoes of the cities and lived completely unto themselves. There they had their own religion, their own law, their own language, their own customs, their own diet, their own economy. Since they were nowhere at home, everywhere was equally home to them.

The early European nations felt the Jew to be as totally alien as he felt his surroundings to be. The Anglo-Saxons, the Goths, the Lombards, the Franks, all despised the usurious infidel. A popular rhyme of Gothic times portrays the three estates as the creation of God, and the usurious Jew as the creation of the Devil. Crusaders on their way to the Holy Land carried out wholesale massacres of Jews. Every European king at one time or another robbed the Jews and drove them from his domain. For 400 years the Jew was shut out from England. When he was allowed back, centuries more passed before he acquired or wanted civil rights of Englishmen. This persecution of the Jew that went on for 1,000 years took different forms -- robbery through forced fines, extortion, exile, massacre -- and it has had one determining, unchangeable result: it has reinforced in the Jew his original hatred for Christian civilization to the point where it is the sole content and meaning of his existence. This hatred is the breath of life to the Jew. He wants to tear down everything which surrounds him, every Western form of life, every Western idea. For a thousand years he cringed before the European master, who was so unassailable in his superiority. The figure of Shylock, drinking his gall and biding his time, taking his usury and saving the coins which represented to him the means of his liberation -- this is the symbolic figure of the Jew for a thousand years. This consuming hatred on the part of the Jew is one of the most important facts in the world today. The Jew is a world power. How did this come about?

THE RISE OF THE JEW TO POWER

It was the Industrial Revolution in Europe and America which enabled the Jew, from having been Shylock for a thousand years, the despised and cringing usurer, to become the type of the modern Jew, the cinema dictator, the tyrant of the inmost thoughts of 100,000,000

Americans. The Jew had been thinking in terms of economics and money for a thousand years before Europe and America began to develop a money civilization. Consequently when money stepped out as the supreme force, the Jew shot upward like a meteor. There was still a barrier however to his complete conquest of power. The heathen, the outsider, was still barred from civil rights. Of old he had not sought them, but now they were necessary if he was to conquer the master of yesterday. Nation after nation succumbed to the principles which the butchers of the French Revolution preached, and which the Jew took up and excitedly shouted over the world. A money civilization wants no aristocracy to stand in its way, so Money and Jew preached equality. Nor must there be any barriers to the employment of money, so the Jew preached liberty. He sought to lose his mark as outsider, for in his new role he wanted to be accepted as a member of whatever nation he might be among, so that he might conquer the power for his revenge. So he preached fraternity for others and the brotherhood of man.

But his "equality" meant only a new inequality -- the dictatorship of the Master of Money over the economic slave tied to his bench with a wage-chain. His "liberty" meant that the Jew was free to squeeze out the life-blood of nations through usury and financial dictatorship. The "brotherhood of man" -- that meant that the Jew was to be accepted as an equal -- but that he was to maintain his ancient unity and desire for revenge. Now the point has been reached where he steps out and asks for special privileges -- and gets them! Yesterday he denied aristocracy -- today he affirms it -- and he is the new aristocrat!! Did not Albert Einstein, before whom Americans are supposed to bow and scrape, write in Colliers Magazine an article entitled "Why the Jew is Superior"? And did not the white Americans afraid to think for himself any longer, read it and believe?

The Jew did not conceive nor organize modem industrialism. No more did he organize liberalism. But when these two things had become realities, he cleverly insinuated himself into the new social and economic fabric which arose, and he has now identified himself with the rapacious capitalism of the sweatshops and with the dishonest and revolting "democracy" of the type where Tweedledum opposed Tweedledee, and the Jew cares not which wins for he nominates them both.

There was a great danger to the Jew in this removal of all barriers between him and the host nations. This danger was assimilation of the great mass of Jews. If this were to occur, the Rothschilds, Baruchs, Frankfurters, Rosenmans, Guggenheims, Schiffs, Lehmanns, Cohens -- all these would be leaders without followers. They would lose their trustworthy followers who could penetrate everywhere and spread the influence of the Jew. One fruitful source of taxation would be gone. So the word "assimilated" became a term of contempt used by arch-Jews to describe other Jews who were losing their Jewish feelings and instincts. The Jew, with his two thousand years behind him, was faced with a perilous situation. No mere money manipulation could cope with this emergency. In this situation, the Jewish leaders invented Zionism.

ZIONISM AND THE PINNACLE OF JEWISH POWER

It was a political master-stroke on the part of the Jew to bring out the movement known as Zionism. Its ostensible aim was to seek a "national home" for the Jew, a plot of ground to which all Jews would theoretically return and there settle. Since the idea seemed to be to make the Jews into a nation like America, one with geographical boundaries, it seemed a praiseworthy movement to Americans. It seemed to promise the end of the Jews as the shifting sand dunes among nations, and to herald their establishment as a civilized nation. Hence unlimited Zionist activity and propaganda could be carried on among the Jews by their leaders, and no suspicion was aroused in the minds of the host nations.

But the real aim of Zionism was merely to save the Jew, wherever he was, from assimilation by the Western peoples, the European and American people. It enabled their leaders to unite the Jews firmly, to prevent assimilation by giving the Jews a political aim to follow. The spurious quality of the movement is shown by the fact that almost no Jews were moved to Palestine. A few only were moved, for commercial and political reasons and to conceal the Zionist fraud, but the millions remained in America and Europe. The real aim of Zionism -- to reaffirm and perpetuate the solidarity of the Jew -- has been successful. Zionism has become the official policy of the Jewish entity, and its ascendancy means, as far as the simple, ordinary Jew is concerned, that he is an utter slave in the hands of his leaders. It is probably superfluous to mention that no leading Zionist has gone from his position of power in white America back to Palestine. Nor need it be pointed out once more how few out of the millions of Jews driven from Europe have gone to Palestine. Almost to a man, they have come to America, their land of promise, the last base for their power, the last place for their revenge.

The invasion of Palestine, strategically important though it is, nevertheless stands in the shade of the vast invasion of America. During the short half century since Jewry adopted Zionism, some ten millions of Jews have been dumped on the shores of North America to displace Americans biologically and economically, to live parasitically on the American organism, to distort the social and spiritual life of the nation. The volume of the invasion has been such that even the slumbering, politically-unconscious white American has begun to blink his eyes and look around him in amazement, as he becomes gradually cognizant that his native land has passed into the possession of scheming, power-hungry, money-grubbing, total aliens.

The alien has his own press, in which he reveals those things which the democratic-liberal press dutifully conceals at the behest of the Jew. Pick up at random an issue of the "Contemporary Jewish Record" -- that for June 1941. On page 282 we are told how Jewish educators are combating successfully "the un-American movement of 100% Americanism". On page 259 a member of the American Jewish Committee joyfully reports that because of the hostility between American and Jew the successive waves of Jewish immigrants "will develop into a cohesive American Jewish community". The article "The Jewish Emigrant -- 1941", describing the arrival of the Jew in America, says: "Our sole conclusion is that when the emigrant has finally arrived at his destination, he can consider himself at the entrance to Heaven".

Seven million of these immigrants have arrived at their "entrance to Heaven" since 1933. There is admitted hostility between them and their host-people. The Jew opposes 100% Americanism. Yet he calls his arrival here his "entrance to Heaven". How is this?

THE RISING INFLUENCE OF THE JEW IN AMERICA

The North American continent was discovered, explored, cleared, plowed and settled by the individual imperialism of members of the European-American white race. The political independence of America was won, and the industrial-technical system of the continent was planned and built by the white race. The American merchant marine was built and sent into the seven seas by white men. Every creative idea in whatever realm -- political, economic, technical, religious, legal, educational social -- that has been brought forth on this continent has originated with, and been developed by, members of the white European-American race. America belongs spiritually, and will always belong, to the Western Civilization of which it is a colonial transplantation, and no part of the true America belongs to the primitivity of the barbarians and fellaheen outside of this civilization, whether in Asia Minor, the Far East, or Africa.

And yet, even though the Jew was not present at Valley Forge, even though he was not at New Orleans in 1814, nor at the Alamo, nor at Bull Run or Chancellorsville, nor at Guantanamo Bay or Manila, even though he took no part in the conquest of the continent -- in spite of this complete dissociation of the Jew from the American past, it is a stark and gruesome fact that America today is ruled by the Jew. Where Americans hold office, they hold it at the pleasure of the Jews and use it in deference to his policy. Baruch argues with Roserman on the steps of the White House -- once the residence of Washington, Madison, Adams -- and the policy of America is thus determined. LaGuardia calls Lehmann by a Yiddish term of abuse in public. As lawyer, the Jew brings in excessive litigation; as judges he imports chicanery into the administration, and has the power to pronounce rules of law for Americans. A rabbi states: "The ideals of Judaism and the ideals of Americanism are one and the same," And the "Jewish Chronicle" (April 4, 1919) says: "The ideals of Bolshevism are consonant with the finest ideals of Judaism". The notorious rabbi Wise announces, "I have been an American for 67 years, but I have been a Jew for 6000 years". The "Jewish Chronicle" tells us: "The Jews in America are 100% Jewish and 100% American". These schizophrenic percentages resolve themselves into the thesis of the rabbis that Judaism, Trotskyist Bolshevism, and Americanism are one and the same. The synagogues have a parade of liberals -- sub-Americans with defective instincts -- come before them to parrot back at them their own view-point.

The Jew numbers approximately 10% of the North American populations but in the Second World War, a war fought solely for Jewish interests, a war of his fomenting, a war to increase his power, the conscripts in the American Army were only 2% Jewish, according to official records. Neither in his assumed role of American, nor in his actual status as member of the Jewish Culture-State-Nation-Race-People, was he willing to risk his blood, even in his own war. In the fighting forces he limited his participation to the administrative branches: Judge Advocate, Medical, Quartermaster, Finance. In the American Army Jewish conscripts have an unconditional right to a furlough for Passover, for Yom Kippur, for Rosh Hashanah. The induction of Jews into the Army is delayed over Jewish holidays -- "to avoid undue hardship". The Central Conference of American Rabbis in the 47th annual convention in New York addressed a resolution to the American Congress asking that Jews be exempted from conscription "in accordance with the highest interpretation of Judaism"!

In the publicly supported educational institutions for higher learning, the Jew is driving out the native American student. In the free universities, such as Wayne University and City College of New York, the Jew's possession is complete. The Stock Exchange presents a similar picture. The New York Exchange is dormant on Jewish holidays. The Officers Reserve Corps is ever more penetrated by the

Jews. The police forces of the large cities are under his control, and the Federal secret police enforce his bidding. He commands the National Guard in the populous states.

How has this come about? How has the native American been driven from the positions of representation, of power and respect in his own land? How has he been chased out of the professions, out of government, of the universities, out of the sources of public information? How did the interloper from Asia, the ghetto-creature from Kishnev, attain to his eminence whereupon he holds in his hands the decision of war or peace, and decides who are America's friends and who are America's enemies?

Two things are responsible for this situation in which America finds itself serving as a mere tool in the hands of an alien. First is Liberalism -- the enemy of national greatness, the virus that eats up national feelings. Liberalism is the doctrine that everyone is equal, everyone acceptable, the doctrine that the botched, the misbegotten are equal to the strong and the superior, that there are no foreigners and no distinctions. Liberalism gnaws away at the structure for which patriots and great leaders gave their lives and fortunes. To Liberalism, America is a "melting-pot", a dump heap for the world's human refuse. When the white race in Europe drives out the Jew, he goes to America where weak heads and inferiors who are jealous of that to which they are not equal have laid down for him the red carpet of Liberalism, and on this carpet, the Jew has advanced to supreme power in the short half a century since he first discovered that America is a fine host for an enterprising parasite. Liberalism is the inversion of that 100% Americanism which the Jew hates.

But mere Liberalism alone does not account for it. The second factor has been the aggressive unity of the Jew, his cohesiveness born of hate, which has welded him together and organized his forces for his mission of destruction. By virtue of the cohesiveness of the Jewish entity, at once Culture, State, Nation, People, Race, Religion, and Society, the Jew conquered the cinema industry, the news-gathering associations which controls all "news" and journalistic opinion, the periodical and book press, and the radio networks. When it became obvious the "Republican" party was about to lose the 1932 election, he cleverly insinuated himself into the "Democratic" party, and placed his candidate in the Presidency. This was the Revolution of 1933, but since it had occurred in the form of a simple change of parties, the politically-unconscious American remained unaware.

In 1933, there descended upon Washington the swarm led by Baruch, Lehmann, Morgenthau, Frankfurter, Niles and Rosenman. In their train were thousands of Paswolskis, Messersmiths, Lubins,

Berles, Fortases, Lilienthals, Cohens, Ezekiels, Silversteins et al, and bringing up the procession came enough lesser Jews, deracinated liberals, technocrats and aliens to double the population of the capital city within a few years.

Between the cracks in the pavement the Jew recruited a thousand sub-Americans as "radio commentators", newspaper "columnists", and professional propagandists to disseminate the world-outlook the Jew considered appropriate for the American. A multiplicity of government bureaus came into existence, necessarily staffed with Jews. The Jew sought to bring under his control every factor of public expression and influence, thus to make sure that never again would there be a free national election for he did not intend to relinquish his power, so long dreamt of, and now at last real, through the free play of any constitutional game of parties and majorities. He purged the central government of whoever could not be led by the nose, or bought. Who opposed was shouted down, smeared with vile labels, and so silenced.

Thus America was given a semitic countenance.

THE WORLD IN FLAMES
An Estimate of the World Situation
By *Francis Parker Yockey*
(Published February 1961, a year after his death)

In October 1946, in a quiet garden in Wiesbaden, an unknown person, whose writings and actions are only valued by his enemies, and that negatively, composed a short monograph entitled "The Possibilities of Germany", and this Estimate can best begin by a short citation from that unpublished work: "Eventually -- not before 15 years, not more than 30 -- the Anglo-Saxon-Jewish combine and the Russian Empire will wage the third of the series of World Wars." 1960 was the first year in which the world political situation was ripe for a great war. But the exact moment of its outbreak is known to no one at this time, not even to any clairvoyant. It may take place this year, or any year after this, the last possible time being about 1975.

I

A brief comparison is in order with the situation of 1946. In that year, America-Jewry controlled, in a political if not military, sense the entire Western Hemisphere, all of Western Europe except a part of Germany, all of Africa, all the Near East, the Middle East, and the Far East. This all amounted to 9/10 of the surface of the earth and more than 3/4 of the earth's population.

Since then, this preponderance of power vi-a-vis Russia has dwindled to a point where the Washington regime at this moment has no preponderance of power vis-à-vis Russia, but stands in an inferior power-position.

The basic reason for the diminution of power is spiritual-organic. Power will never stay in the hands of him who does not want power and has no plan for its use. Desire for revenge, desire to "stop Hitler", desire to destroy Europe, and desire to kill 80,000,000 Germans by the Morgenthau Plan -- all these are not will-to-power. Will-to-power means inherently the will to do something positive with that power, not the will to prevent something.

The more superficial and direct reason for the diminution of power was political incapacity on the part of the Zionists, or Washington regime as it is here interchangeably called. This incapacity manifested itself first in total incomprehension of the Russian soul, leading to the belief that this wild, chaotic; spirituality had surrendered itself permanently to the guidance of a small group of Jewish intellectuals.

A person who believes that the seizing of the apparatus of power -- government, army, police, press, education -- guarantees the continuance of power is a political non-entity. Yet the whole Washington regime believes this. In philosophy they are materialists and thus cannot ever understand that visible facts are only the manifestation of invisible spiritual movements.

To the extent that a people are materialistic in its religion and philosophy, it is non-revolutionary, but the Russians are completely non-materialistic, being completely dominated by feelings, and acting always from their feelings. Thus it was that the Russians, even without disturbing the Bolshevik governmental structure or ideology, affected a complete revolution and deprived the Jewish leadership of all power. The Jew in contemporary Russia is allowed to be a Jew, if he is first and foremost a Russian. In other words he is not allowed to be a Jew, and is being exterminated without physical violence.

Since the Washington regime believed in the "friendliness" -- i.e. Jewish domination -- of Russia, it gave China to Russia, as it had already given part of Germany and part of Japan. One cannot call this treason on the part of the nincompoop Marshall who accomplished the actual transfer of China from the Washington regime to the Russian sphere, for he was sent by the Washington regime on this very mission, and when he died, years later, was called by the Zionist press the greatest soldier, etc., etc. Legally speaking, it makes no sense to say the entire government of a country is committing treason, for it is they who define the enemy. In a spiritual sense, of course, the Washington regime are traitors to the United States and its people, but they have so defined the relationships that those who are loyal to the United States in a spiritual and political sense are regarded as traitors in a legal sense.

India was surrendered in 1947, and lost to the control of the Washington regime. Together with China it accounts for about 40% of the world's population.

Since then, Egypt has been lost and half the Arab world, through the creation of the foolish, unnecessary Jewish State in Palestine.

Cuba and Venezuela have been lost, with only financial bridgeheads retained, and all the Latin American possessions of the Washington regime, from Nicaragua to Argentina, are growing restive.

Because it retained the fiction of the independence of the European lands, the Washington regime has imperilled its grip on France, by allowing De Gaulle to set up himself up as a leader.

In Korea, the Zionists fought against the Chinese armies they had created, through the Great General Marshall, and these armies used the very equipment which Marshall had delivered to them, sufficient to equip 60 divisions. Not only did they lose the war, but they demonstrated to the entire world that the United States infantry is inferior, and that the Zionist empire is, in the Chinese phrase, a paper tiger.

On the positive side, there is little to record. The Zionists conquered Spain without a war, and have occupied it with their troops. They have completely incorporated England, and occupied it once more with troops.

Of all that they possessed in 1946, there remain only the greater part of Latin America, (now precariously held), all Europe except part of Germany and the greater part of the Mediterranean littoral (also precariously held). Japan has been lost, but Australia, without military value, is still held. The Philippines are still precariously held.

What the Washington regime has lost Russia has gained, either by extension of its influence directly or by increasing the neutral area. The extension of neutrality is of immediate benefit to Russia, exactly as it is of immediate loss to America-Jewry. This is so because of the concentric shape of the geographical theatre of the political struggle.

Russia occupies an inner circle, and America-Jewry an outer circle. The neutralization of India, Japan, Egypt et al. represent breaks in the outer circle, and weakening of the Jewish-American economic-political structure.

This is so also for a moral reason. Jewry always claims to speak for, and to represent, all humanity, with the exception of one unit, which is thus automatically the enemy of humanity. In a war of attrition, it is a positive detriment to be labelled by most of the world's press as the enemy of humanity, even though in a short war it makes no difference. Therefore, the more the Jewish-American control over the press of the countries of the world is weakened; the better is Russia's moral-political position.

II

It is instructive to compare the Second and Third World wars in their aspect of the quantitative relationships of the combatants. In the Second World War, on the one side (Germany, Italy, Japan, Hungary, Finland, Rumania and Bulgaria) were 225,000,000 people, with an area of less than 1,000,000 square miles at the beginning of the conflict. On the other side were approximately 1,000,000,000 people and approximately 50,000,000 square miles. In addition the so-called neutrals (with unimportant exceptions) were enrolled in the economic service of the Jewish-American-Russian coalition, since the coalition possessed a monopoly of their trade.

In the distribution of 1960, the quantitative aspect looms thus: on the one side of the Jewish-American leadership is a population of 400,000,000 and an area of approximately 30,000,000 miles. (These figures include all North and South America, all Western Europe, and more than half of Africa, together with Australia and environs.) On the other side of the Russian-Chinese coalition is a population of 800,000,000 and an area of approximately 15,000,000 square miles. (This includes Russia, China, and the Russian-held areas of Europe.)

These quantitative estimates are generous to the American-Jewish front, for much of what is given is questionable, from the standpoint of military value of the population and accessibility of the territory. Thus it is quite clear that none of the armies in Jewish-American occupied Europe will have great military value, since the essence of the armies, i.e. morale, will be absent. Furthermore, the entire population of Latin America is at best available only for economic service; there is no expectation that in the Third, any more than in the First or Second World Wars, this population can be used as cannon-fodder. And if the movement for Latin American independence spreads, almost a third part of the figures, both for population and land area given above must be stricken. If the Arab revolt spreads further, it may cut off much of Africa from Zionist control.

On the moral side, the two wars are quite different. In the Second World War, Germany and Japan were both nationalist. Only secondarily, and in a propaganda way did they claim to represent any principle which was of universal validity. Thus they offered no great persuasion to the population in enemy countries or neutral countries to sympathize. The Jewish-American-Russian-English etc. etc. coalition, however, used no nationalist feelings except as propaganda against Germany. Their whole war cry was a universal one: Freedom, Happiness, Justice; a birthday-party every day for every person in the world.

In the Third World War two universals are offered by the contestants: on the one side the joys of Capitalism, on the other the perfect happiness of Communism. Germany, Italy and Japan all got out of the League of Nations when it was clear that it was entirely dominated by the enemy. Russia stayed in the United Nations all through a long period when the thing was entirely Jewish-American, and has persevered to the point where the thing can be sometimes useful to them even though they do not have the major control.

Thus, while the United Nations was at war against Russia's ally in Korea, a Russian was the head of the Security Council, the organ charged with the prosecution of the war.

A national, or particular, principle against a universal principle is at a crushing disadvantage in a World War. But this time, the Zionists face another Universal, and one with which half of their very own people are secretly, half-openly, or openly in sympathy. In a wax between Capitalism and Communism, the Jewish people finds itself physically on the one side, but spiritually on the other. Their minds are divided from their pocketbooks. This weakens leadership corps of America-Jewry, for this corps is entirely Jewish. The Jewish-American entity is Jewish as respects its head, American as respects its body.

In view of the complete lack of spirituality, intellect, political awareness, and moral courage in the American population, the possibility of an American revolt against Jewish domination has been entirely omitted. Such a thing is only a possibility after America-Jewry suffers a thorough military defeat, and even then only if it is followed by large-scale economic disasters.

III

The regimes of Washington and Moscow together make up a Concert of Bolshevism, just as the Culture States of the West made up the Concert of Europe of the 18th century. Moscow and Washington share all basic values, and recognize it mutually. No matter how strong their political rivalry, they make "cultural" agreements whereby each may export its brand of culture to the other. Thus Washington sends the clown Bob Hope to Russia, and Moscow sends the cacophony expert Shostakovich to North America, causing the intellectuals to gush with admiration. The American cinema is not anti-Russian, regardless of preparations for the Third World War. Compare this with the preparations for the Second World War, when this same cinema created many thousands of hate-Germany films, which it is still turning out.

Bolshevism means, as simple historical fact, destruction of the West and of the remnants of its Culture. The Communist Manifesto sets forth a program to accomplish this on the economic-social side. In the ten demands that it makes, only nine are possible, and all these have been realized in the United States, but not one of them has been realized in Russia. The barbarian nature of the Russians is itself Bolshevism, but Marxian Communism is purely an export article in Russia, while in the United States, it is an accomplished fact.

The reality of this Concert is shown especially by the Policy of America-Jewry toward Germany. Much as it needs a German Army, it will not create a real German Army, but only a mass of helpless rifle-battalions to be slaughtered by Russia without a chance of winning. Both Russia and America-Jewry have failed to get the best performance from their German captives who make the rockets for them. Russia overworks its German rocket-men, and America-Jewry has so thoroughly denationalized, brain-washed and Americanized its German rocket-men that they are no longer German, and have thus lost the source of their technical superiority, i.e. their German inwardness. This is the final explanation why the German rockets made in Russia are better than the German, rockets made in the USA.

Most of the cinema in North America treats Russia and Russians as interesting and admirable, human and good. The cinema's purpose in the general scheme of propaganda is to control the emotional attitudes of the population. Control of the intellectual attitudes is the work of the press, and here Russia is treated negatively. Why this duality? Every ruling regime gives perforce in its propaganda a picture of itself, and the Washington Zionist regime itself suffers from this quality. Russia is not a total enemy, but a rival. The Korean war, 1950-1953 expressed the limited hostility of the Washington regime toward Russia and its official war-aim was not "victory" or "unconditional surrender", but "a just truce".

When the Germans in Russia make some new technical advance, Eisenhower congratulates the Moscow regime. Roosevelt never congratulated Hitler on such occasions. The Russian flag is flown in the United States on all festive, "international" occasions. Never did the German flag appear, nor does it today. The fundamental ineradicable Jewish hatred of Germany appears in the fact that even the Germany they control directly is not permitted to sit among the United Nations, on a par with the other puppets. The spate of anti-German films in the theatres and on television continues unabated. The anti-Russian films are few indeed,

One conclusion emerges, of military-political significance: in the Third World War, the Washington regime will list Germany among its enemies. Already the radio propagandists say "Russia and Red Germany." The intention here is not only that the German rifle battalions be slaughtered by the Russian advance, but that the way be opened for the bombardment of Germany again, this time with more destructive bombs.

The Concert of Bolshevism is a reality only because of the attitude of the Washington Regime. Russia does not disturb it, since it works to their ends -- it gave them China, neutralized India and Japan. But they do not take it seriously, any more than they regard the United Nations as a serious thing.

138

IV

We now come to the military aspect of the Third World War, It is perfectly clear that the Washington regime has put its entire faith in "strategic bombardment." They plan to deliver the explosives to their targets by ballistic missiles, guided missiles, submarines and airplanes, land-based and carrier-based. This faith in bombardment is just that: it is faith, but not rational. Faith has certain advantages, but not in the realm of technics. Belief that I will discover a new weapon, will or at least, may, lead me to that discovery, but belief that this weapon will destroy my enemy all by itself will not increase the power of the weapon. Black magic would be better in this case, for it works directly on the morale of the enemy, whereas the faith in the weapon merely assumes that if his cities are destroyed, he will be disheartened.

Russia is a porous target, and rockets are effective only against dense targets. The Jewish-American citadel is far denser than the Russian citadel, and is thus vulnerable to rockets to a far greater decree. America-Jewry would be better off if rockets did not exist. In that case its citadel would be inviolate, and it could never sustain a military disaster of the greatest magnitude, for its armies would be at the antipodes and their victory or defeat would be of minor consequence. Thus the basic Jewish-American military doctrine is one which cannot possibly give it victory. But this same military doctrine, if adopted by the enemy, could give victory to the enemy.

Russian morale is tough, because of the barbarian nature of the soldier-material, and not because of good leadership, organization, or indoctrination. The Jewish-American morale is poor; the soldier material is utterly worthless in itself. This population has no political awareness, no significant military tradition, no military instinct, no military ambition, and no moral strength, and no respect for, or belief in anything whatever. This youth is characterized by the Beatnik, the American form of the Nihilist. He believes in nothing and respects nothing because there is nothing within his range of vision worthy of respect or inspiring belief. The Beatnik is not an insignificant entity: he is the ruling type in the American youth. He represents the fashion; all other youth feel inwardly inferior to him, as non-fashionable elements always do toward the fashion-corps.

Russian barbarians cannot be demoralized by rockets. The Beatnik can, because he has no morale to start with, no inner participation. The Russian population is young, and it is rural, mostly in fact, the rest in spirit. The American population is old, and it is megalopolitan, mostly in fact, the rest in spirit. Speaking in general, only rural people are good fighters, not city-people, especially if the fighting is severe.

Rockets are merely artillery, and thus can never conquer. It is true that the doctrine arose in military circles during 1914-1918 that "artillery conquers the ground; the infantry occupies it." But this is mere stupidity, on a level with the military leadership and conduct of that war. Only infantry can conquer.

From this fact comes the Russian military doctrine. It derives from Clausewitz and is valid for all wars between powers based on the same continent. That doctrine is that the aim of war is the destruction of the enemy's armies by decisive blows. The Russian military sees in the Jewish-American bombardment of German cities in the Second World War mere stupidity, and here they are correct. But this same Russian military has not yet fully grasped the fact that the Clausewitz doctrine on The Aim of the War is not valid for intercontinental warfare. As far as the Jewish-American puppet armies in Europe go, the doctrine is correct. For Russian victory in Europe, these puppet armies must be rounded up, as they inevitably will be. But there still remains the Jewish-American citadel. How is Russia, without massive means of sea-transport as it is, to destroy the Jewish-American armies? It is simply not possible. Does this mean therefore that Russia cannot win?

It is clear that both contestants in the Concert of Bolshevism have a ruling military ideation according to which they cannot possibly win.

America-Jewry, which believes in rockets, can win only with infantry. Russia, which believes in infantry, can win only with rockets.

So much for their similarity; now for the difference. Although the ruling doctrine in Russian military circles is an infantry-oriented one (as it should be), nevertheless the Russian military has equipped itself with good German rockets, better than the German rockets of America-Jewry.

But the Military of America-Jewry, though it talks out of one side of its mouth about "balanced forces," has not equipped itself with good infantry, for the simple reason that it cannot, entirely lacking any human material which could be shaped into good infantry. The Jewish-American naval forces now have the doctrine that they are mere artillery auxiliaries. The submarines exist to throw rockets; the carriers exist in order to carry airplanes to throw rockets; the cruisers exist to -- yes, why do they exist? Away with them, to the mothball closet! The naval battle at sea, the meaning of the fleet, is not contemplated. Protection of commerce is forgotten, since overseas commerce will almost all be cut off in the Third World War.

The Russian forces are prepared to fight with infantry, with artillery, with armour, with air forces, with missiles, ballistic and guided, thrown from land and from submarines. The American-Jewish forces are prepared to fight only with rockets.

Since the rocket is the only Jewish-American weapon, it is understandable that they do not want to abolish atomic weapons, nor to agree to stop their further testing and developing. By the same token it is understandable that the Russians sincerely want to render illegal the only weapon which America-Jewry can use against them.

But here only the Russian position is rational. The American-Jewish position would make sense if (1) it could win with rockets, and (2) it had superiority in rockets. But neither condition is present. It would be better to get out of the competition before the war than to lose the war, but politicians in general do not think that way.

The dispute rages in Russian military circles on whether American rocket manufacturing, storing, and launching facilities should have top target priority, or whether that should be given to American cities. Those who think nationalistically, organically, patriotically, humanly, would attack the rocket facilities first; those who think in terms of cold reason, regardless of domestic damage and losses, would attack the great cities as the prior targets.

V

Now, it has been said that America-Jewry can win only with infantry, and that Russia can win only with rockets. These propositions must be fully explained.

First, the meaning of the concept to win. Immediately the political and military planes separate themselves out. Politically, the concept of winning means the conclusion of peace on terms satisfactory to one's self militarily it means that the enemy asks for peace.

This does not contradict Clausewitz in his statement that the military aim of war is the destruction of the enemy's armies. It merely widens the concept of military victory to cover the case, which arises now for the first time in world-history, in which a war is fought between two powers whose armies can have no contact with one another.

This assumes that in the first phase of the war the Jewish-American forces in Europe and their local auxiliaries will be entirely destroyed or expelled from Europe, including England of course. A minor series of operations will follow, hardly to be called a phase of the war, i.e. the finishing of the complete domination of Asia by Russian or Chinese arms. This will include the occupation of Hong

Kong and Singapore, the neutralization of Pakistan, the occupation of Persia, the conquest of Turkey, and the delivering of the Jewish-American puppet formations in the Near East to the United Arab movement. A small-scale war may also be necessary to clean out completely the Jewish-American bases in North Africa. Japan will be neutral or allied to Russia.

But after this phase, the issue of victory remains undecided. The Jewish-American regime will not surrender, since the very existence of Jewry is at stake, and the whole United States and its population is there to secure the existence of Jewry.

So here is a war between continents whose armed forces have no contact, nor can they have any contact. Russia has no possibility of delivering a large army to the North American continent, Nor is it possible for America-Jewry to deliver a large army to the Eurasiatic continent, first because it has no such army, nor can it raise it in the numbers and quality necessary, and second, because it is impossible to mount an invasion of Eurasia from the North American continent.

Thus the only "contact" the hostile armies can have with one another is in the limited form of an intercontinental artillery duel. By these means, it is possible for neither contestant to destroy the armies of the other, since these will be widely deployed, offering no target. The only real target for intercontinental ballistic missiles is a large city. Here the United States offers a plethora of targets, and Russia few.

What is the effect of Jewish-American bombardment of Russian cities? And what is the effect vice versa? The Russian is a peasant, whether or not he tills the soil. He, is not city-oriented, even when he lives in the city. When the city is destroyed, little is destroyed, so he feels, The American, and *a fortiori* the Jew, is a megalopolitan, whether or not he lives in Megalopolis. When the city is destroyed, all is destroyed, so he feels. He who reads may draw his own conclusion at this point.

Next is the question of bombardment at intercontinental range by guided missiles. Since their precise degree of accuracy is a secret-secret-secret-secret matter, only common sense is available. Common sense teaches first that at thousands of miles distance no rocket can be guided to say, a factory, or within destructive range of it, and second, that against every weapon, even superior weapons, defences, even if not complete and perfect, are always worked out. It would appear that guided missiles will be simply an auxiliary to the basic artillery, namely ballistic missiles, and will thus not be decisive.

Next is the question of bombardment by bomb-carrying aircraft. After the first phase of the war, the heaviest Jewish-American aircraft will have to take off on their bombing missions thousands of miles from their targets in Russia and Germany. These targets will be Russian rocket factories, stockpiles and launching facilities, as far as they know where these are located. On this point there is no doubt whatever that Russian counter espionage is many times as effective as that of American-Jewry. There is also little doubt that Jewish-American espionage in Russia labors under almost invincible handicaps. Thus, these aircraft will not be too well supplied with targets, and will not be decisive.

What was said above about bombardment at intercontinental range by ballistic and guided missiles applies equally well to bombardment at continental ranges by the same type of missiles, launched from ships of all types. And what was said about land-based bombing aircraft applies still, even though with less force, to bombing aircraft based on, aircraft-carrying ships. These have a shorter distance to travel, but since they cannot destroy something whose location is unknown to them, such airplanes are no more dangerous than Jewish-American espionage makes them.

On the point of bombardment by aircraft, Russia is thus better situated by virtue of the superiority of its espionage, and the relative inferiority of the counter-espionage of America-Jewry. But the fact that they have few if any aircraft carriers means that their aircraft must fly thousands of miles before reaching the target.

We come back to the city as the target. If bombardment of cities is not decisive, no other form of bombardment will be decisive. But it is quite clear that only in the case of America-Jewry can bombardment of cities even possibly be sufficient for a decision to ask for peace.

If this happens, an interesting new possibility opens up. In November 1918 Germany surrendered to the English-led coalition, consisting of England, France, Italy, Japan, China, India, Portugal, USA, etc. But after the surrender, England continued the blockade, a war-measure after the war. Since the war was over, this could not be called a means of destroying the enemy's armed forces. It was solely a means of killing civilians, and in this blockade, continued until July 1919, a million people died of starvation in Germany.

Now England was a civilized power, yet it continued war after surrender of its enemy. There is thus the distinct possibility that barbarian Russia, signatory to no treaty to mitigate the harshness of war, would continue to bombard USA after a surrender, in order finally to eliminate it as a potential world-power, by complete destruction of its industrial potential (which is almost entirely in cities). That which the Jewish-American-English-French forces did in

Germany after the Second World War; destruction of industrial plants, and irrational plundering of natural resources in order to destroy them, could be equally well done by Russia after the Third World War: further destruction of cities, perhaps occupation (large armies might no longer be necessary) to destroy industry systematically, on the pattern used by American-Jewish forces in Europe 1945-1950. If there were no occupation, the forest areas could be destroyed by systematic bombardment, converting most of the North American Continent into desert.

VI

The foregoing has assumed that Russia and China would be able completely to occupy the Eurasiatic continent. How far is this assumption justified?

At present the Russian army is in a class by itself, being the only large army in existence which is fully equipped with the best weapons and of good fighting quality. The Chinese army is large, not fully, equipped, not equal to the Russian in moral qualities. The Jewish-American army is quite inferior in size to both its enemies, extremely well equipped, but of poor fighting quality. The German army is small, entirely without equipment, entirely without morale. The Turkish army is small well equipped, and of good moral quality. The Italian and French armies are both small, ill-equipped and without morale. The English army is small, well equipped, and without morale. The Spanish army is small, not well equipped, but of good morale.

In a war between a coalition and a single power, the single power will win if other conditions are equal. A coalition must outweigh a single power. The coalition forces against Russia in Europe, however, are vastly outweighed by Russia in addition to their decisive handicap of being quite lacking in fighting morale.

The only army in the coalition of the Jewish-American forces in Europe which can be expected to fight well is the Spanish. The terrain in Spain also favors a defender. If De Gaulle is able to consolidate his regime he may neutralize France, and, as already seen, neutrality works for Russia. Not only France would be affected by such a development. Neutrality is the wish of all the peoples of Europe, and this force will definitely reach the political plane if it's given the encouragement of an example.

While it is possible that the Jewish-American forces might be able more or less to stabilize a front in France, in Spain, or in Turkey, this possibility is abstract at this moment, for the armies are neither in existence nor in a position which could stop a Russian invasion force.

Thus, the assumption that the first phase of the Third World War will develop as outlined above is one justified by the conditions of 1960.

No estimate would be complete which leaves two great political developments out of account, both of recent years. The first is the Arab Revolt, led by a great and vigorous man, Gamal Abdul Nasser. The second is the formation of nationalist, neutralist regimes by such brilliant statesmen as Marshal Jozef Broz Tito of Yugoslavia, Nehru of India, Field Marshal Ayub Khan of Pakistan, General Ibrahim Abboud of the Sudan, Sekou Toure of Guinea, Sukarno of Indonesia, Nkruniah of Ghana, and others. These personalities embody an Idea; none are out for money or publicity. They live simply, work for and live for their ideas. One such man, in a position of leadership, is a world-historical force. All lead weak political units, and cannot by themselves fight either of the great world-powers. But all want independence for their people; Nasser, for example, for some 300,000,000 Moslems. Each is a symbol to great human masses. Their significance, in each case, in this Estimate, is that they diminish the Jewish-American power without augmenting the Russian-Chinese power. By their Palestine policy, the Zionists may even succeed in driving the Arab world to fight for Russia.

Eventually responsible leadership for a restive mass of some 180,000,000 Latin Americans will evolve. Already the seeds of revolt against Jewish-American economic domination have been sown. Witness Cuba.

The growing tide of neutralism in the world, is due to the political incapacity of the leadership corps of America-Jewry. If this tide rises in Europe, America-Jewry would be defeated before the war. De Gaulle is not a great man, but if he is able to gain French independence, he will immediately find himself the spiritual leader of all Europe, pygmy though he is. De Gaulle is a cretin, but people will follow even a cretin if he embodies their deepest, most natural, instinctive feelings. De Gaulle's driving force is a vanity of super-dimensional extent. Even Churchill, the embodiment of the Idea of Vanity itself, was still content to be a Zionist executive with a front position, a big office, and a resounding title. But De Gaulle wants more: he wants to be equal to the masters who created him and blew him up like a rubber balloon. Because of the spiritual force upon which he has accidentally alighted -- the universal European desire for neutrality -- he may even succeed. An idiot might save Europe. History has seen things as strange.

VII

An unusual point among the historically-unique relationships of the Third World War is that while neither side can win -- in the classical military meaning -- neither can lose, in the classical military meaning of that word. The armies of America-Jewry cannot destroy the armies of Russia, and the armies of Russia cannot destroy the armies of America-Jewry on the North American continent. Into the middle of an Age of Annihilation Wars comes now a war in which political and military annihilation is mutually impossible to the contestants.

But in a political sense, victory is still possible. Victory means, in the Third World War, not annihilation of the opponent, but conclusion of peace on one's own terms. Speaking thus of political victory, it is clear that America-Jewry -- under the conditions of 1960 -- must lose, and Russia must win.

Russia holds the initiative, it has the moral force, it has the arsenal. America-Jewry has no moral force, completely inadequate military forces, and has moreover a military doctrine (or, perhaps, an anti-military doctrine?) according to which it does not need any military force except artillery.

This Russian pre-eminence is not at all owing to Russian cleverness but solely to its opponent's stupidity. To cite once more the unpublished "Possibilities of Germany" from the year 1946: "In every respect but one, Russia is superior to the enemy. Technically, America-Jewry is better prepared. The only way Russia can overcome its handicap in this respect is through German brains. In a word, Russia needs Germany." Since 1946, Russia has obediently armed itself with such rockets as Germans have made for it, and this has been its main cleverness.

It was not Russian cleverness which drove out Chiang from China, but the Jewish-American agent Marshall. Russia did not neutralize India -- The Anglo-American troops there were withdrawn by order from Washington. Russia did not occupy Eastern Germany -- America-Jewry gave it to Russia. Russia did not take the Suez Canal -- Nasser did it. Russia did not liberate Cuba -- Cubans did that. Russia is not making trouble in France for America-Jewry -- that is being done by De Gaulle, and the Communist party there has opposed him to the utmost. The Russian Communist Party in the Western European countries harms the Russian interests, and merely serves as scapegoat, bogey, and whipping boy for the Washington regime.

Russian "successes" -- except for its German-made rockets -- are all the gift of the Washington regime. Jewish-American political stupidity is invincible. But the power-gifts which the Washington regime has made to Russia are not explicable entirely by simple stupidity, simple incapacity. There is the further factor at work that the Zionist Washington regime is on both sides of most power-questions in the world. Its sole firm stand is its fundamental anti-German position: Germany must be destroyed; its young men must be slaughtered. In Algeria, Washington is on both sides: it is with the French Government, as its "ally": it is with the rebels by virtue of its world-program of "freedom" for everybody. In Egypt, the Washington regime told Palestine, England and France to attack, and when Russia rose, it told them to stop. It was, within a week, anti-Nasser and pro-Nasser. It occupied Lebanon, then evacuated. It held back Chiang when from his island; he would have attacked China with whom the Washington regime was then at war. It defended South Korea, but helped the Chinese maintain their supply line to the front. During the Chinese War in Korea, it made war and negotiated peace at the same time, for years. In Cuba it forbade exportation of arms to the loyal Batista and thus helped Fidel Castro; now it is committed to the overthrow of Castro.

It is a psychological riddle, decipherable only thus: the Zionists have two minds, which function independently. As Zionists, they are committed to the destruction of the Western Civilization, and in this they sympathize with Russia, with China, with Japan, with the Arabs, and as such they anathematize Germany, which is the mind and heart of the Western Civilization. As custodians of the United States, they must half-heartedly remain at least the technical and political domination of that Civilization even while destroying its soul and its meaning. In a word, they are working simultaneously for and against the Western Civilization. Quite obviously they are thus doing more damage than conferring benefit! If a commander of a fortress sympathizes with the enemy, but yet insists in defending the fortress rather than surrendering it, he has surely found the highest formula of destruction.

Thus the newspaper tag of "East versus West" is meaningless. It is East versus East, with the West supplying the lives and treasure for destruction.

If Russia represents the Principle of Stupidity, then Zionism represents the Principle of Malice. Of course neither of the two is without the leading characteristic of the other, but stupidity reigns in Moscow, and Malice in Washington.

The orchestra is in the pit, the spectators gape uncomprehending, the curtains rustle with expectation. The play is entitled "Where Ignorant Armies Clash by Night." Stupidity is in the lead, supported by Malice. The producer is Destruction, and the company is called The Forces of Darkness.

It is already the predetermined curtain-time. Will the drama commence on time?

Francis Parker Yockey (1917-1960) on his way to the prison in which he would be found dead.

Also Available from Invictus Books
www.invictusbooks.com

Imperium
Francis Parker Yockey
$25.00

This is Yockey's famous masterpiece. It is inspired by Oswald Spengler's Decline of the West. Imperium advocates the creation of a pan-European empire governed by sound principles or 'absolute politics'. It is divided into five parts, which are concerned with History, Politics, 'Cultural Vitalism', America and the World Situation. Imperium deals with doctrinal matters as well giving a survey of the 'world situation' in the 20th century. "In this book," writes Yockey, "are the precise, organic foundations of the Western soul, and in particular, its Imperative at the present stage." "...What is written here is also for the true America, even though the effective America of the moment, and of the immediate future is a hostile America, an America of willing, mass-minded tools in the service of the Culture-distorting political and total enemy of the Western Civilization." "The mission of this generation is the most difficult that has ever faced a Western generation. It must break the terror by which it is held in silence, it must look ahead, it must believe when there is apparently no hope, it must obey even if it means death, it must fight to the end rather than submit. ...The men of this generation must fight for the continued existence of the West..." "The soil of Europe, rendered sacred by the streams of blood which have made it spiritually fertile for a millennium, will once again stream with blood until the barbarians and distorters have been driven out and the Western banner waves on its home soil from Gibraltar to North Cape, from the rocky promontories of Galway to the Urals." The book's Chicago-born author, Francis P. Yockey, was just 30 years old when he wrote Imperium in six months in a quiet village on Ireland's eastern coast. His masterpiece continues to shape the thinking and steel the will of readers around the world.

THE MYTH
OF THE
TWENTIETH
CENTURY

An Evaluation of the
Spiritual-Intellectual
Confrontations of Our Age

ALFRED ROSENBERG

The myth of the twentieth century
Alfred Rosenberg
$24.95

The Myth of the Twentieth Century was one of the principal ideologues of the Nazi. It was the most influential Nazi text after Hitler's Mein Kampf. The titular "myth" is "the myth of blood, which under the sign of the swastika unchains the racial world-revolution. It is the awakening of the race soul, which after long sleep victoriously ends the race chaos. In this, his seminal work, Alfred Rosenberg offers the reader a genuine alternative to the political and spiritual attitudes which modern Western society leads us to believe are our only options. From every center of power today we are told that we MUST accept democracy as the only "good" form of government, that we MUST choose either the Judeo-Christian tradition, the New Age movement, or secular humanism as our faith, and that we MUST look to either Adam Smith or Karl Marx for economic wisdom. In "The Myth of the Twentieth Century," Rosenberg takes aim at all of these assumptions and presents us with a worldview entirely different from any of those based upon them--one with its roots deep in those primeval affective, aesthetic, and intellectual inclinations characteristic of the Caucasian race. He argues powerfully for an organic polity as opposed to a Universalist one--most specifically in the Germany of his time--but more generally for Western Civilization as a whole. At the heart of his argument is the provocative thesis that each of the races of the human species possesses a different kind of "soul," which is the origin of human cultural diversity. Environmental influences cannot account for the differences in style and achievement among the races, he argues; the respective environmental conditions under which they have lived have been far too similar to admit of such an explanation. Advancements in the scientific understanding of genetics made since Rosenberg's death, moreover, lend weight to his thesis and make it well worth a thoughtful look. "The Myth of the Twentieth Century" will be of interest to those searching for their identity and its significance amid the anomic trends of contemporary Western life, as well as those looking for a socially relevant philosophy with some depth as an alternative to Establishment prejudices and platitudes.

A National Socialist Life
George Lincoln Rockwell
$12.99

Rare and hard to find essay's, poems and articles by the founder of the American Nazi Party (ANP) Commander George Lincoln Rockwell. Some never before published! With an inspiring biography and Eulogy for the assassinated leader of the ANP titled "A National Socialist Life" by Dr. William Pierce the author of "The Turner Diaries".

The Holy Book of Adolf Hitler
James Battersby
$12.99

THE HOLY BOOK OF ADOLF HITLER, is called by many the Bible of neo-Nazism and of esoteric Hitlerism. This powerful work not only examines the successes and triumphs of Adolf Hitler, it additionally provides an inspiring template for the reunification of the West under the banner of a strong, pro-White government that will not bow down to the forces of money or jews. The history of the Germanic peoples are traced back into antiquity, the contemporary problems of the day are examined in an even light, and the corresponding destiny of the people of the West is laid bare for all to see. There are two parts to this book 'The German Revelation' & 'The Book of Aryan Wisdom and Laws'. Battersby covers many different topics explaining Germany's role and what was really happening during WWII. This is a must read for students of National Socialism. "For the Germanic peoples true religion is founded in race." First published in Britain in 1952.

20515504R00088

Made in the USA
Middletown, DE
29 May 2015